BUTTERFLIES & COALSMOKE

By the same author

Beyond the Dictionary in Spanish (1953; 1972)
Cassell's Colloquial Spanish (1980)

BUTTERFLIES & COALSMOKE

A. BRYSON GERRARD

Susan Abrahams
Oxford

First published in Great Britain by
Susan Abrahams Limited 1988

Acknowledgement
I owe a great debt of gratitude to Henry S. Harvey, the onlie midwife in the delivery of these insuing recollections, whose tireless attention both to structure and to detail, as well as encouragement in moments of gloom, did more than I deserved to make my offspring presentable to the public.

ISBN 1 871155 00 2

Typeset in Palatino 10/12 by Columns, Reading
Printed and bound in Great Britain by
Dotesios Printers Limited

For Kane and Levi Grant, who, at the ages of four and seven respectively, provided so many reminders of what it means to be a young boy.

Contents

Romford Revisited

One day in 1982 I took the two little boys to whom this book is dedicated to a Railway Centre where, among other pleasures, we could go for a short ride in the old-fashioned compartment of a train drawn by a steam locomotive – a 4-6-0 of the 'Hall' class. They'd never been in a train before so I told them how one put one's luggage up in the rack and, if the journey was a long one, walked along the corridor for a meal or else got out one's sandwiches and had a picnic in the train, en route for a holiday, say in Scotland. Their intense interest set me recalling the world I inhabited when I was their age and prompted me, when not long afterwards I found myself in London's City with time on my hands, to go and have a look at Romford, my birthplace, unvisited for six decades and for me the centre of my young world.

I was at once struck by the fact that Liverpool Street Station was a great deal cleaner; when I was a schoolboy its walls were black with soot and I was surprised to discover that the Victorian building had been, and was now again, red brick. Another striking difference was that many of the railway personnel were also . . . I was going to say 'black' but I mean West Indian or Pakistani. The railwaymen of sixty years ago though racially 'white' were often very much blacker, thanks again to coal, and a good deal poorer and more proletarian too. The gulf between the classes was deeper and less bridgeable then. Advertisement was also now less clamorous than formerly. In the old days, in each arch of the sooty brick archwork which formed the side of the station there'd been a large enamel plaque: PEARS, PEARS, PEARS, PEARS . . . which tried to stun one with the virtues of Pears Soap, and on every riser of the steps up to the booking office smaller plaques, enamelled white on blue, had proclaimed Mazawattee Tea, Mazawattee Tea, Mazawattee Tea . . . until one was nearly dizzy. Now they were no longer there and no one has heard of Mazawattee Tea. On the sides of the platforms larger plaques had forced one's attention on Mellin's Food, or a large pen nib with the legend 'They come as a boon and blessing to men, the Pickwick, the Owl and the Waverly Pen'. Even out in the country, hoardings in the fields, about 100 yards from the line, would remind one of Beecham's Pills, or Carter's Little Liver Pills. Within the compartments of suburban trains glazed advertisements extolled the virtues of Scott's Emulsion, Dr Scholl's Foot-easers, or Dr Collis Browne's Chlorodyne. This hucksterish hard-selling was so usual that my parents were little conscious of it whereas children, when they can first read, read everything and ask questions about it.

The Great Eastern Railway was an important fact in my young life. I was born on it, so to speak, and, similarly speaking, every inhabitant of the kingdom was born on some line or other. The railway was basic to Victorian life; for all classes the normal way of getting about. Even the wealthy few who could afford a horse and carriage would only use it for short journies. As early as 1848 Dickens has the wealthy Mr Dombey being 'whirled along' in a train to Birmingham, and notes that 'everything around is blackened'. What he does not mention, and I suddenly noticed as absent in 1982, was the smell of coal smoke and its concomitant soot; so all-pervading that, like Mazawattee Tea, it was written off, although chronically there. It must have been the most characteristic smell of the Victorian era. Coal was the all-but-universal means of heating and cooking, and such a constant demand meant a constant supply so that an auxiliary smell was that of the coal-yard; a tweedy, brackeny, ammoniac smell associated with railway sidings where 'goods trucks' stood, piled high with Derby Brights, Anthracite, 'slack' and the like. That ammoniac smell permeated the clothes of the coalman when he came to deliver the stuff, humping a shiny, black hundredweight-sack of it onto his back and, bowed with the weight of it, walking slowly up the garden path, across the yard, and emptying it into the coalshed.

The exit from Liverpool Street in 1982, therefore, through what had formerly been a Doré-esque inferno of tunnels and bridges permanently fogged with smoke and its bitter aloes smell until one emerged at Bethnal Green, was very much cleaner and less disagreeable. Beyond Bethnal Green a strong smell of paint had formerly exuded from the 'Robbialac' factory and, once past Bryant & Mays, one had been in the aura of 'Isinglass' manufacturing glue and gelatine from fish bones and emitting a stink which took a minute or more to get through. Now the train slipped electrically along with odourless, chuffless ease, past Stratford (no longer the Great Eastern's locomotive works), past Maryland Point (now simply Maryland), past the huge cemetery at Manor Park (still there). Coming out of Ilford station very much *not* there was the Ilford Super Cinema which had been such a landmark and an influence but before I had time to consider just what that influence was we were already slipping through Seven Kings, Goodmayes, Chadwell Heath, all with associations and food for thought. We even slipped easily and undelayed into Romford and this, by the standards of sixty years previously, seemed surprising. Romford station had presented its Victorian engineers with a problem; it had to be on an embankment and also to cross South Street, hence almost on a bridge. All the way from London there'd been two pairs of lines, one pair Fast, the other Slow, but since a bridge wide enough for four tracks and platforms would have been a great deal more expensive they'd decided to reduce them to two, with the result that lengthy stops outside the station, while waiting for a Fast train to get through, had been almost normal for Slow trains.

The Romford station yard of my childhood had had a long ramp which formed the pedestrian approach to the Down platform with a line of hackney cabs drawn up alongside it. At the top of the ramp was a glass-canopied staircase with a balustrade down the middle of it which we used as a slide while waiting for Father's train to come in. Meeting him at the station had been an excuse for a 'walk'. When not thus engaged we used to talk to the ticket collector and one day were startled to find not a man but a woman! This remarkable innovation, we gathered, was due to 'the war'. She wore a cloth cap and was a good deal more formidable and less talkative than her male predecessor. It didn't occur to us that she might feel self-conscious about her revolutionary role and so on the defensive.

The horses in the cab-rank were each supplied with a nosebag to keep them happy while waiting, and the cabmen had clearly developed almost personal relations with them and were acutely conscious of their needs. When not trotting with their fares the horses remained standing in the shafts and I used to be struck by their way of resting one leg at a time by lifting it, clopping it gently on the cobbles with an ironclad toe, and leaving it poised on tip toe while the other three legs took the weight. Those constant single clops were one of the chief features of the mostly silent yard. Another feature was of course horse-dung, and not only of station yards but of streets and roads everywhere. Men or boys cleaned it up with dustpan and brush and deposited it in metal containers by the roadside. These were emptied from time to time and the dung was sold for manure but the smell of horse-dung, though it had been characteristic for centuries, too familiar to be noticed for most of the time, was another which was now missing. The same applied to the sound of horses' hooves. The very surname Smith is too common to be noticed yet the fact of its commonness tells its own tale. There'd been a smithy just off South Street between Ind Coope's brewery and the yard of the Crown, behind Barclay's Bank, and the clink of its hammer had been a feature of that neighbourhood, with children staring while the smith hammered the shoe into shape on the anvil, doused it in water and then – it seemed amazing that the horse usually raised its foot in readiness! – hammered it on to its hoof.

I didn't expect to find it there in 1982. Most of South Street was unrecognisable. Even the Congregational Church, an important landmark in my young life, had gone, and South

Street had quite a different set of smells, chiefly cooking smells from the numerous West Indian and Pakistani shops. Its atmosphere was more 'East End', but a latterday East End, much more honky-tonk, which brought the realisation that the Romford of my childhood had been to a large extent a quiet Essex market town. The blacksmith's clients had by no means all been cabmen; farmers from miles around had also brought their horses there for shoeing, especially on market day, and Romford market had been an institution for centuries. Every Tuesday men would rope together lengths of open fencing to make pens for cows, sheep and pigs, and coops for ducks, geese and chickens, and on Wednesday mornings the animals were all herded into them. The cattle had mostly been herded along the roads and cowpats and sheep droppings told of their passing. Pigs and poultry, however, came by cart – sometimes even by van – and getting the pigs in and out of them was a noisy and none too gentle business; the men frequently dragged them down the wooden ramps by their tails and ears while they squealed their protests at the top of their bent and we children stared and giggled.

Two of the farmers, members of that now-vanished Congregational Church, had been friends of Father's and we were sometimes invited to tea at their farmhouses, with scones and cakes made by the farmer's wife. One was Mr Mann whose farm was in Petit's Lane, just beyond the Cottage Hospital, and whose lands extended down to the lake in Raphael Park. It was only a ten-minute walk from our house in Western Road. The other was Mr Fowler whose farm was at Collier Row and so a very long walk. There was no public transport but Mr Fowler had a pony and trap and invitations to tea there usually meant that his eldest daughter, Bessie, only a year or two older than I, would come clip-clopping along to our house to take us there. Mr and Mrs Fowler were both Scottish and spoke with strong Scottish accents so tea there meant oat-cakes and drop-scones with butter from their own churns. Jam, of course, was made from their own home-grown fruit.

'Of course' because this was almost universal; practically everyone, including Mother did the same. Jam-making was one of the year's rituals and most of the fruit was home-grown, almost the sole exception being Seville oranges for marmalade-making in January. Blackberry jam or jelly came from fruit picked in the local hedges, usually down the further reaches of Petit's Lane, and picnics with blackberrying in view were one of the pleasures of September. By and large people still lived closer to the land and were much more conscious of what it could produce; it was unusual to buy factory-made jam in a shop. 'Bottling' fruit, such as plums or pears, to provide dessert courses in winter, was another annual ritual and it was normal to have a larder, or other cupboard, in which to store it all. Canned fruit – or tinned, as we mostly called it – certainly existed but was regarded as something of a luxury, at all events in wartime. Before refrigeration came in, fruit and vegetables were far more subject to seasonal availability and exotic ones such as peppers and aubergines were unknown. Even grapefruit, which came in after the war, was a curious novelty, a sort of cross between an orange and a lemon which one wasn't quite certain how to handle.

During the war 'home'-growing became a patriotic activity and 'home' could mean any little patch of ground that could be exploited, including railway embankments which were not too steep. When a building site became available in Junction Road, beside the stream which backed the houses in Eastern Road, Father took an 'allotment' and made us almost independent of the shops. Articles would appear in 'the papers' on how to make the most of them and give instructions on the making of 'potato clumps' for storing them in winter. We were even encouraged to grow tomatoes; not a very satisfactory outdoor crop in England but they could be ripened in the window and the many green tomatoes at the end of the season could be used for 'green tomato jam', or of course chutney. One day, I suppose around 1917, Father read out of the paper a recipe for using stinging nettles as a vegetable with the result that Mother, my sister Pen, and I, each armed with gloves and a pair of scissors, worked through a nettlebed at the side of the allotment and came back with what seemed a huge bagful though it boiled down to a much smaller quantity of something resembling spinach. Eating it at once made clear that unless the nettles were very young they were stringy and the dish was not accounted a success and not repeated, despite shortages. In 1982, however, the nettlebed had become part of somebody's front garden. As for Petit's Lane, it was already being built up in the 1920s and even before we left Romford I remember being indignant that a favourite picnicking spot had been gouged through to make the 'Southern Arterial Road', i.e. what is now Eastern Avenue. By that time, too, Mr Fowler had accepted a handsome offer for his valuable building land in Collier Row and retired a wealthy man. He'd been one of the first of our acquaintance to buy a car, a sure sign of wealth in the days before mass production.

Western Road, Eastern Road, and Junction Road which connected them were the uninspired names of residential roads which had been laid out in an uninspired piece of town-planning in the 1870s, each of them dead straight, on land that had once belonged to Francis Quarles, the seventeenth-century poet – or so I gathered from Father, and as his own father's house had been one of the first to be built in Western Road (in 1880) he probably spoke from definite knowledge. Their dead-straightness had been relieved by planting trees along each side so that by the time I knew them they might reasonably have been termed 'avenues', but in contemporary photographs of them not a vehicle is to be seen. Traffic, in those days, was confined to such things as the milk cart which came clopping along each day with its tall brass 'churn'. In 1982 they were lined with parked cars on both sides, and streaming with moving ones down the middle so that I was chiefly conscious of a chronic restlessness. The traffic never stopped.

This is now so normal everywhere that, like the coal smoke of the past, it ceases to be noticed; if I hadn't been so aware of the Western Road of sixty years previously I shouldn't have noticed it myself. In the past things were not only quieter but more tranquil and the purpose of a residential road was to serve the houses which lined it. Now, despite the fact that many of the houses were still identifiable, they no longer seemed really residential, each house a home and a castle. A high percentage of the rooms in them would certainly be bed-sitters. The road had become the main point, with the houses as an incidental background, instead of the other way round. Front gardens had been removed to make room for the sacred car or, where not so removed, were overgrown and neglected.

The house where I was born, built in 1903/4, my home and castle for the most formative years of my life, was just recognisable; a semi-detached whose other half had been occupied by Uncle John, Father's brother, and Aunt Elsie, Mother's sister, and their children, Isabel and Sandy, cousins close enough – since we had identical grand-parents – to be almost brother and sister to us, so that their half had been equally familiar, within as well as without. Now the two halves had been joined to form the premises for a solicitor's business, and the two front gardens paved over to make room for several parked cars. Through the front window I could see typists sitting at typewriters in what had once been our Edwardian drawing-room with its cretonne sofa, its upright piano, its Chinese screen and, in the window, an aspidistra on an ebony table. Within it young men from the artists' Rifles camp at Gidea Park had sung their songs – 'Shipmates o' Mine', 'Trumpeter, what are you sounding now?', 'The English Rose' – on wartime Sunday evenings. In the bedroom above had been Mother-and-Father's brass bedstead and a marble-topped washstand with basin-and-ewer, soap dish and other pieces of bedroom crockery all of the same pattern.

Next to Uncle John's half had been a rather larger, detached house with a neat carriage drive leading to a vast garden with a bowling green, a tennis court, a sizeable orchard-cum-kitchen-garden. I associated it with 'Mrs Barrett' and great crops of greengages and Victoria plums with the bloom still on them and an indescribably rich smell/taste when one bit into them which Elgar's music can still recreate alive. Now it was an untidy car-park with unkempt buddleia and michaelmas daisies – and no Red Admirals or Painted Ladies – at its edges, and the drive had become a rough track. Walking along it and passing what had been Aunt Elsie's kitchen I found myself recalling 'Monkey Brand', 'Old Dutch Cleanser', 'soft soap', the mangle with its wooden rollers, and the smell of chloride of lime, put down to bleach the sink. Now, no doubt, it would be where the typists made their coffee. Our former gardens were partly covered by an extension to the solicitors' premises, the rest being overgrown and neglected fruit-trees. The spacious gardens on each side of us had always made me regard ours as rather small but I now realised that although long and narrow they were large by present-day standards. If people lived closer to the land in the past it was partly because, in relation to the population, there was more land to be close to. The gardens on each side of us had had the attention of gardeners but Father's 'small' strip had been enough to produce annual crops of currants, raspberries and gooseberries, and the overgrown fruit-trees had included two sorts of pear – Conference and Beurre Hardy – and four sorts of apple – Worcester Permaine, King of the Pippins, Blenheim Orange and Cox's Orange – and thanks to his careful pruning they cropped very well. One year the Cox had broken one of its branches with the weight of fruit. The general impression given by the present was one of neglect and indifference but it may have been due to the knowledge that the whole neighbourhood, being so close to the town centre, was scheduled for demolition. It would then no doubt become a desert of high-risers and people would live off other people's lands elsewhere.

Eastern Road presented much the same picture as Western, I walked along it chiefly out of curiosity to see whether my first dame school, 'Miss Newman's', was still standing and was surprised to find that it was; a yellow-brick, three-storey semi-detached 'villa' with stone mullions round its windows and front door. One day there, in 1916, Miss Newman had introduced a lady with instructions to call her 'mademoiselle' and telling us that she was a 'refugee' from Flanders (my parents later explained what a refugee was). We were much taken aback at the almost incomprehensible way she spoke English but we already knew the French to be our Gallant Allies and were duly sorry for her. Her French lessons chiefly consisted in teaching us the Marseillaise and I'd learnt to sing it in faultless French and in complete ignorance of what the words meant. It was many years before I realised I'd been singing revolution.

'Miss Newman's' disinterred other memories less flattering to my self-esteem. I was discomfited to recall that at one point I'd tried to persuade nearly all the other children to show me their private parts though in fact most of them obliged, some willingly, others more secretively. One pretty little girl, a doctor's daughter, although quite willing, felt that privacy was necessary and led the way to the house next door which was empty – and now demolished – so that the laurel bushes in its front garden were overgrown. Hidden by the bushes she gaily pulled down her knickers and not only demonstrated but for good measure did a pee.

Romford market-place had suffered less depradation than I'd feared. Parts of it were still quite recognisable and I suddenly realised that it had always formed the background to certain imagined scenes, particularly, for some reason, in 'Russia'. This must have been due to seeing pictures of events in Russia around the time of the Revolution. Except on market day it was a vast expanse of cobbles and I probably equated it in my mind with what is now Red Square, another – rather vaster – concourse (was it also cobbled at that time?). In 1982 however, hardly a shop bore the same name even if the pubs did. *The Pig in Pound* was a name that had arrested my attention as a child though it was years before I realised it was a pub; it was on the wrong side of the square and we never passed in front of it. Pubs were places that the middle classes seldom entered. My parents regarded them with something like horror and most of Romford's were in any case of the 'spit and sawdust' variety. The poshing up of pubs started, if I remember rightly, in the 1930s when they were becoming increasingly 'tied' and brewers had a vested interested in making them more respectable.

One Romford pub which had escaped much of this opprobrium, even in my young days, was the Golden Lion and as it was now lunch time I decided to use it. I couldn't compare it with the past as I'd never been into it before but guessed that it would then have had a Saloon Bar, a Public Bar, a Private Bar, and probably a Smoke Room too. I seemed to recall a side-entrance in North Street that had been labelled *Public Bar* and was 'spit and sawdust'. The main building had eluded censure partly because it was also a hotel but also because it was old and traditional; an old half-timbered coaching inn, in fact, with an overhanging first floor on the North Street side. Mother had told me one day that it was 'Elizabethan' and, watching the draymen rolling the wooden barrels in and out of its cellars and the maids cleaning out the rooms I became aware of a much older England of the sort depicted in 'Little Song of Long Ago' under 'Dame, get up and bake your pies'.

By now, of course, it was 'open plan' with uniform prices, and quite a number of those using it were young men, some with 'punk' hair-dos. This was surely another difference with the past; the young can seldom have been seen in pubs as they never had any money; nowadays they often form the majority. There was also a juke-box, another indication of youthful clientele which provoked the thought that pubs in the past, like the streets outside them, will have been very much quieter places than they are now. The only 'music' I'd associated with them, or the streets outside them, was drunken singing heard on Saturday nights.

Sitting at a 'ploughman's lunch' and looking across the street outside – in so far as traffic permitted – reminded me that Austen's, the draper's, was no longer in existence. Freddy Austen, the draper's son, had at one time been something of a buddy and had come home from school on the same train. GER suburban trains had then consisted of separate compartments, corridor trains being confined to long distance, and as our schools finished before the rush hour they were seldom crowded. Schoolboys invariably looked for 'an empty' and when they found one all manner of vandalism and misbehaviour was possible, especially with boys en masse. At the various stops down the line, however, they got out in ones and twos, things became quieter and misbehaviour could take other forms. By the time we reached Chadwell Heath they'd nearly all got out and Freddy was the only other besides myself who went as far as Romford but, as the Chadwell Heath-Romford stretch was a longer one, and usually further protracted by a long wait outside Romford to let an express through, there was time on one occasion for Freddy, who was circumcised, to demonstrate his quite unusual technique for 'tossing off'. As we were both rising eleven it was only to be expected that we should be interested in the exciting novelty of masturbation and therefore in comparing notes. Sex was too interesting for most boys to be much inhibited by parental taboos about it, but this thought, entertained in the Golden Lion in 1982, provoked the further one that Elizabethan schoolboys with their satchels, returning willingly from school, must have done much the same.

Although in Great Eastern territory, Romford didn't escape the tentacles of the Midland Railway and in this it was by no means unique; the Midland might turn up anywhere. Most of the 'Great' railways – Eastern, Western, Northern, Central – stemmed from London, and even the Great Northern, despite this title, reached no further north than Doncaster where the North Eastern took over. The Midland, however, though it later penetrated to London with a small terminus at St Pancras, was far more wide-ranging and the centre of its network was Derby. From there, first on its own account, and later by buying up smaller companies or negotiating running powers, it penetrated from coast to coast and into Wales and Scotland. As a result it acquired quite a different personality from the other lines, and one much enhanced by its crimson livery, both for engines and carriages. Those dusky red trains could turn up in Norfolk, Cumberland, Dorset . . . it would be quicker to name the few shires where they didn't turn up and they coloured my very earliest recollection of 'trains'. I must have been about three when Mother went to see an old friend of hers – 'Aunty Jessie' – in Manchester and took me with her, on the St Pancras line. She said it was 'the most comfortable line' and this was evidently received opinion. I recall little of the journey except that it seemed enormously long – I suppose about four hours – but my mind photographed the upholstery; deep crimson coarse velvet with a pattern of interlocking isoceles triangles, and with no wooden bar along the front of the seats (and so under childish bare knees). Despite being ill-remembered, however, the journey has that mythological quality of memories which half-emerge from the oblivion of early childhood, and red trains can still furnish the odd dream.

The Midland had penetrated into Essex by buying up the London, Tilbury and Southend Railway (in 1912) and my childhood journeys on it normally went no further than the next station, Emerson Park, where from the age of six I daily went to school, at first in the company of Pen, but thereafter alone. Its Romford station adjoined that of the Great Eastern but had had a separate entrance on the other side of South Street; a vast echoing booking-hall with one tiny booking office at ground level and a wide, majestic flight of stairs up to its one wooden platform between whose planks I once found a Puss Moth 'asleep' and promptly added it to my butterfly collection.

I was pleased to find the platform still there in 1982 but the approach to it was now via the ex-GER station and the booking-hall site had been put to other uses. The trains, of course, were no longer Midland red; they were blue and white British Rail – and pretty down-at-heel – but at least they still ran so I boarded one to see how Emerson Park compared with its former self, hoping on the way to see the fields across which we'd walked when we missed the train, or when there was a strike. The fields had belonged to Great Gardens Farm which, like the Fowlers' at Collier Row, can still furnish the background to a novel when 'a farm' is mentioned. The fact that I could recall it in all weathers suggested that we must have missed the train pretty often, or else walked for preference; it was only two or three miles. I recalled picking dog roses in June, woody nightshade in July, seeing a threshing machine with a traction engine to drive it at harvest time, swedes and mangolds being dug up by 'German prisoners' in winter, and muddy paths in all seasons except when it was frozen hard, or baked hard in high summer. The smell of cow-dung pervaded the farmyard; rather a comfortable smell. By 1982 I didn't doubt that the fields would be covered with houses but was unable to confirm it; the embankments were as neglected as Western Road's gardens and so a riot of trees, bushes, brambles and old-man's-beard which completely blocked the view. Perhaps the inhabitants of the houses were glad to have the railway hidden but in the days when everyone took a pride in it such negligence would have shocked the railwaymen themselves.

Emerson Park, a suburb of Hornchurch, had started life as a somewhat up-market housing estate of Edwardian vintage and its planners had not confined themselves to the rectilinear; its main thoroughfare, Parkstone Avenue, was a succession of deliberate curves. Hornchurch itself had been barely more than a large village and Miss Jones, the very ladylike dame of our dame-school, lived only about 500 yards from its centre, yet during the summer of 1917 she'd got permission from the local farmer for us to have a hay party in the fields opposite her house in 'Spikey Terrace', Butts Lane, (so called because the top front of each gable was adorned with a wooden spike). Traffic being in those days almost negligible we mostly walked along the middle of the road which had barely been made up and consisted of tarred granite chips levelled by the grinding and trampling of a steam-roller. There were often muddy puddles in which we splashed about, an irresistible temptation for children wearing Wellington boots. The opposite side of Butts Lane had been hawthorn hedge practically all the way to Butts Green and beyond. One dark, clammy November morning, near the corner of Parkestone Avenue, we'd met a small boy with a Union Jack in his hand and, exercising our right of seniority, asked him what he was carrying it for. 'War's over', he said, but the way he said it suggested that he was repeating something he'd been told and was as uncertain as we were about the real significance of the words. 'The war' had been going on for the whole of our conscious lives and we needed the authority of grown-ups to confirm that something important had happened. It was not until the next day, when we turned up at school at the usual time and were greeted at the door by an excited Miss Jones saying 'I think we'd all better have a holiday' that its importance was really brought home to us.

In 1982 there was no question of splashing about in muddy puddles; the middle of the road was streaming with incessant traffic and I was again struck by the way the road seemed to hog the scene. Everything was subordinate to it. Another part of rural Essex had been turned into subtopia; not so much a place as a transit camp, with its sense of neighbourhood much reduced. Part of Spikey Terrace was – surprisingly – still there but instead of having fields opposite it had a view of houses and shops, and fairly squalid shops at that, with a smell of stale fat about them, as if deep-frying were the only form of cooking known there. The only other reminder of the past was an iron notice-board mounted on a short length of railway line, painted black with a notice in white lettering announcing that the land was the property of the London, Midland and Scottish Railway. This was just outside Emerson Park Halt, and somewhat hidden by overgrown bushes, but it seemed a wonder that some railway buff hadn't pinched it. British Railways would hardly have cared, surely, even if they'd noticed. In the days when the railways did care, a high percentage of stations had gardens which the staff tended when business was otherwise slack, and made many of them perfectly charming. During the war they'd often been used for growing vegetables. Emerson Park's embankments were too steep for horticulture but I recalled trying to catch an Orange Tip on them one bright day in May. Now they were likewise overgrown. Had railways, in their day, reduced the sense of neighbourhood? Reflection suggested that they might have increased it by making people – for the first time in many cases – aware of other neighbourhoods, though still far enough apart to maintain their difference and feel proud of it.

As it was a mere 'halt' I rather expected that by 1982 it would have dispensed with the tiny booking-hut which was formerly there but no, there was a somewhat larger hut with more of the air of a booking-office. During the war a boy had been in charge of the old one – he can't have been more than about twelve – and when I'd had a long wait and there was no one else on the platform he used to invite me into the hut to talk. Although I was three or four years younger I was at least somebody to talk to, and he could show off his manliness; he used to demonstrate blowing smoke out of his nostrils. On one occasion he broke off conversation and without a word walked out of the hut. When I looked out to see where he'd gone I saw him standing on the edge of the deserted platfrom and pissing across the single line of rails in a huge arc (the halt boasted no Gents). He came back without comment and conversation was resumed without reference to the interruption but I was aware that sex lay only just below the surface. That it never in fact surfaced was probably due to shyness, no doubt complicated by class-awareness. Age-awareness was yet another factor; he would have regarded me as a mere kid while, for me, he seemed almost grown-up.

That our conversations ceased was due to the end of the war. Demobilised soldiers wanted their jobs back and boys were no longer needed. I regretted his going. Although quite ignorant of the facts of life I'd somehow sensed that there was something more about sex that I needed to know. Going back to Romford in the train that day in 1919, staring at the fields of Great Gardens Farm and wishing that sex had surfaced between us had brought me to the thought: what could we have done and where would it have got us? The thought was somewhat guiltily entertained at the age of eight since everything to do with sex was taboo but I nevertheless entertained it and it probably had something to do with a tendancy to associate sex with the working classes. Other childish contacts with them had come via Sunday School and the Boys' Brigade whose 1st Romford Company Father had founded. Both had been important influences and seemed to deserve closer investigation, indeed the day's outing had made it clear that there was a suprising amount of retrievable material about 'the past' tucked away. When the blue-and-white British Rail carriages appeared round the curved cutting from Upminster and drew into Emerson Park Halt I inevitably recalled their crimson predecessors, the smell of hot oil from the tank engine's shifting valves, clambering up into a compartment upholstered with those interlocking isoceles triangles, and found myself wanting to tell those two little boys what the 1910s felt like and smelt like. Also sounded like; music insinuated itself by association; wartime 'pop' tunes, the hymns we sang at church, my piano pieces, the tunes they played at the cinema . . . Returning to Romford on the Tilbury line in 1982 l decided to get it down on paper.

Victorian Survivals

The 'Romford' evoked by that 1982 visit had a strongly Edwardian flavour though in fact it belonged to the reign of George V, but periods do not abruptly begin and end with the death and succession of monarchs. I can boast Edward VII's stamp on my birth certificate though he was dead by the time I was born (in 1910). HM Commissioners for Oaths were evidently not going to waste perfectly good stamps just because the image and superscription on them happened to be out of date and used them up before going on to George V ones, but 'periods' are governed by larger considerations and what we now regard as 'typically Edwardian' lasted until the 1914–18 war and in some respects beyond it. Seen from this side of that great watershed it can even seem like the Victorian age carried on by other means; looking back, one can see that what is distinctive about a period takes no account of what remains unchanged from previous periods and when communications were less all-pervading than they are now, pockets of the past could survive more readily.

There was one such pocket in Hornchurch where some friends of Miss Jones's lived: Mr and Mrs Dendy, whose son Dick was also at her school for a while, sometimes invited me to tea. I knew little about architecture but see the house in my mind's eye as early-Victorian enough to suggest Regency, with a wide gravelled drive curving round a lawn up to a pillared front door. Mr Dendy was a shadowy, stern-seeming figure whom I seldom saw but Mrs Dendy was gentleness itself, with a soft, sweet voice, very much a lady and with a band of velvet ribbon round her throat. They had a musical box hanging on the wall of the drawing-room with a picture painted on it, in fact I thought it was a picture, if rather a thick one, until one day she went up to it, did something to it at the edge and lo and behold, a lovely spangle of tune tingled out of it. What left the most abiding impression, however, was a butterfly collection in a handsome cabinet about eight drawers high. As I already collected butterflies and had a book about them I was filled with admiration at seeing Clouded Yellows, Large Tortoiseshells, Greenish-Silver-washed Fritillaries and other treasures, all smelling strongly of moth balls. 'They were all caught in Kent', Mrs Dendy said, and as they included a Camberwell Beauty, which my book had made clear was 'very rare' I thought what a marvellous butterfly county Kent must be though in fact I'd once caught a Bath White – also very rare – in Essex.

The house always seemed to me remarkably silent, probably because at home, what with my cousins next door, there were five children about the place whereas Dick was an only child. I fancy a child of my age who visited such a house now would be even more struck by it. Radio, television, transistors, cassettes, juke-boxes, cars in the road outside and aeroplanes overhead have made silence not only a thing of the past but positively irksome to the young, whereas I, in my old age, find it increasingly golden; the past established a norm which is still valid. It was also a spacious house with a garden large enough to need a gardener, thereby providing a norm of another sort; just as Great Gardens Farm is likely to figure as my mental picture of 'a farm' when I read about one in a novel, so does 'Sutton Lodge' when the background of 'a large house' is required in my mind's eye. Re-reading Elizabeth von Arnim's *Elizabeth and her German Garden* recently I suddenly realised that Sutton Lodge had always been the scene I'd visualized for its setting, with Elizabeth looking very much like Mrs Dendy. Our copy had fin-de-siecle illustrations and they dressed very much alike.

'Sutton Lodge' has acquired a further magic by being associated with the merry month of May and apple-blossom time. 'The sweet of the year' is likely to impinge on everyone as a moment in its own right and I suspect that the reason lies partly 'in our stars', or more strictly our star; it is a moment when that high, bright sun is approaching its zenith, the world is becoming 'lush and lusty' and a sense of 'God is Good' pervades the land. If Lytton Strachey is to be believed, the trees and the grass at Kensington were Queen Victoria's earliest memory, and if this suggests that his own was something very similar he would be far from unique. I could match it with lying in the grass among the daisies – it must have been the spring of 1914 – in Aunt Elsie's front garden with flowering currant and philadelphus scenting the hedge next to Mrs Barrett's; one of those moments of unconscious awareness that can emerge from the oblivion of early childhood with its acute, almost animal sense of smell. By now it is more amply vegetated with bluebells, wallflowers, auriculas, Bleeding Heart, and the scent of Lily of the Valley but the details are local. Many years later I experienced the same sense of elation in Chile, yet there the merry month is November, the high bright sun shines from the north and goes the 'wrong' way round the sky, and the wild flowers are such things as eschescholtzias and certain kinds of flowering tree almost unknown in this country. In old age I find the spring evoking a feeling of almost unbearable sadness, as if it were too beautiful to be borne, too charged with memories, and feel almsot relieved when it fades into the light of common summer, but when I remind myself that my first conscious appreciation of it was at Sutton Lodge in the spring of 1918 I suspect that the memory is unconsciously charged with that Great War which undid us, then at its very worst.

Another pocket of the Victorian past where silence was for the most part golden was our Aunts' house in Croydon. Invitations to stay there were regarded with great excitement, not least because two separate railway journies were involved. The first, from Romford to Liverpool Street, was becoming almost familiar, though still exciting, and it was followed by a bus ride, whenever possible on the upper deck, in those days unroofed so that you got a better view of the river and the Tower Bridge when the bus crossed London Bridge. If it rained there was a small tarpaulin fixed to the back of the seat in front which you could pull over yourself, and we enjoyed doing this; we'd have preferred the upper deck even it it had been snowing! It was in any case not a long journey and ended at London Bridge Station.

In Victorian times there were three separate stations at London Bridge, each belonging to a different railway company. By my time the High Level and Low Level were joined by a footbridge and by the name South-Eastern & Chatham Railway, but the 'Brighton' side, a terminus belonging to the 'London, Brighton, & South Coast Railway', had no connection with them and kept itself severely apart. Although both lines served a good many places in common, a ticket on one line wasn't valid on the other and until the Amalgamation of 1923 you had to make up your mind which you were going to use.

The LBSC had been enterprising enough to electrify some of its suburban lines (in 1909) but although these included East Croydon they were 'all-stoppers' and we never used them. I didn't mind this. Steam locomotives were what interested me though at the time of day when we travelled, London Bridge seldom had anything exciting to offer. The LBSC's best trains – the Brighton Belle and the Newhaven Boat Train – left from Victoria so that I rarely saw those handsome Baltic 4-6-4 tank engines, only the usual hum-drum little tanks with rounded tops. The official livery was 'umber' but in wartime – and most of these early journies were in wartime – nearly everything was a dirty coffee colour.

Details such as these were for the most part observed privately. Mother's only interest in a train was to ensure that it was the right one, though given time enough she could be persuaded to find a compartment which would be near to the exit at East Croydon and, for preference, a seat with one's back to the engine, so that there was less danger of smuts. In the days of steam, railway journies, especially in summer when the windows had to be at least a little open, tended to make one grimy, and on arrival at one's destination it was taken for granted that one would want a wash. Once installed, however, we all took an interest in the views from the window and these were in sharp contrast to those on the Great Eastern. Whereas getting out of Liverpool Street involved passing through an inferno of tunnels and smoke, out of London Bridge one was on high – 'one of the longest brick-arch viaducts yet built' – and much of Bermondsey clustered round its skirts with glimpses of cranes in the Thames docks in the distance. As for factories, the most noticeable was Shuttleworth's chocolate factory just outside New Cross Gate, and the occasional whiff of chocolate aroused no indignation.

After New Cross Gate there was – by Essex standards – 'a terrific hill'; the train chuffed along getting slower and slower. There were times when it seemed doubtful whether it would manage it, especially when the engine's driving wheels lost their grip and went flying madly round until the driver blew a blast of sand under them and persuaded them to grip again. The summit was at Forest Hill after which we gathered speed through Sydenham, Penge and Anerley, Victorian suburbs which seemed to outclass their GER equivalents of Goodmayes, Seven Kings and Chadwell Heath and which in any case had Norwood Junction to crown them. Norwood was a railway 'spaghetti junction' and I used to wonder how the signalmen managed to control it. It was also the last station before East Croydon and therefore surveyed with mounting excitement; we were 'nearly there'.

The Aunts' house, No. 60 Dingwall Road, was just round the corner from the station and they'd lived there since the 1890s. It was not a large house by the standards of the time (only four-five bedrooms) but it had high ceilings as well as a large porch reached by steps with pillars on each side so that it seemed august, and my genteel aunts rather heightened this impression. The youngest of them, Harriet, worked in the Bank of England and so commuted daily to London but her sisters, Pattie and Madge, ran a high-class dress-making establishment, with its title 'Madame Jardine' announced to the world on a well-rubbed brass plate outside the front door. One of the bedrooms had been turned into a 'working-room' where, in the company of seamstress assistants, they spent a large part of their day and sometimes much of the night, only emerging for meals or when a client came for a fitting. Fitting took place in the 'fitting-room' whose walls were adorned with fashion-plates in pen and coloured wash illustrating the *dernier cri* worn by women with impossibly high heels. It was used, when necessary, as a 'spare room'; a curious folding bed with creaky wooden lattice-work sides was unfolded and stretched out (and not found very comfortable by their eldest nephew). When a dress had reached a sufficiently advanced stage, however, fitting – or more precisely 'trying on' – took place in the drawing-room downstairs. This was furnished with two large mirrors in art nouveau frames, one of them hinged to the wall so that the lady could get a back view of herself in the other one.

Mother would sometimes return to Romford leaving me to stay for a few days during which I had time to take in the house and its ways. Within the working-room, on an average day, the main sounds were the depositing of scissors – some of them huge, with handles to fit the whole hand! – on the deal work table, interrupted now and then by the noise of the treddle sewing machine. Behind Pattie's seat there were two tailor's dummies, one slim, the other less so, one of which would occasionally be brought out to hang a half-hemmed dress on and ensure that its skirt was equi-distant from the ground all the way round. Behind Madge there was a cupboard full of treasures: reels of silko in all imaginable colours, little hanks of 'crewel silk', sets of buttons fixed to cards, some of them beautifully enamelled (with fin-de-siecle decadence, and presented to the London Museum fifty years later) as well as lengths of gloriously-patterned 'material'. There usually seemed to be a fire in the grate; ironing was done by flat-irons which needed heating before use. This was always preceded by careful testing, either by holding the iron near to the cheek or by a quick dab of a just-licked finger. Expertise was needed to know the right temperature and one or two burnt silhouettes of the flat-iron on the ironing board told of the acquiring of that expertise. In between all this was a little desultory conversation, or the seamstresses would ask questions about their work and be given careful instructions by

Pattie or Madge. The visits I recall best, and which enabled me to observe this scene, took place when I was about five or six and had recently learnt to read, so that I was put to useful employment by reading aloud to them from 'Alice in Wonderland'.

The view from the working-room was of one side of East Croydon station across a number of shunting lines and a coal yard, and the puffing of trains was often heard. I found these sounds fascinating – they were different from Romford's – but the working-room had been put at the back because of 'the noise' (shunting often took place at night). Their bedrooms were at the front, overlooking Dingwall Road, and although during the day there were the sounds of clopping horses and of Croydon Corporation Tramways, at night they were as silent as the grave. Once when I was there I contracted what was described as 'indigestion' and was put to bed in Grannie's upholstered mahogany bed while work continued in the working-room. For much of the day the only sounds were the striking of the dining-room clock, the musical chimes of the town-hall clock, the grind of the trams in George Street and the occasional clip-clop of a cab or cart. This bedroom and the drawing-room below it had Venetian blinds with wooden slats to exclude not only excessive sun by day but moonlight or lamplight at night. Come twilight these would be carefully lowered but the slats were not close-fitting enough to exclude thin streaks of lamplight from below so that the ceiling was neatly fretted with these. Now and again, in the evening, a cab would pass – sometimes even a car! – and there was then a cross-array of brighter streaks which splayed across those of the lamp in a moving fan-pattern.

One or two of the pictures on the bedroom walls were reproductions of country scenes by Birkett Foster but most of the pictures in the house were original water-colours by their 'Uncle Robert', R. M. Bryson, fairly well-known I was told, in the 1860s and 70s in the Glasgow area. His speciality was landscape and I was a little shocked that he used Chinese White, having been taught – by Miss Jones – to regard this as almost unethical, but I was nevertheless impressed by his professionalism. It was in fact a snowy scene, with much use of Chinese White, which I liked best; youths in drainpipe trousers were blowing into their freezing hands while in the distance was a railway train with a Rocket-type chimney and you could see that it was a 2-2-2. For some reason I felt sure that it was the Caledonian Railway. In the working-room was a spacious cupboard that you could walk into and there the Aunts had bound volumes of Little Folks and Chatterbox of the 1880s. There'd originally been eight sisters and these books were handed on from one child to the next. Since they never threw anything away the Aunts were now able to supply a younger generation with reading matter.

Mother had often told us how their father had died, young and uninsured, leaving them without an income. Grannie, with eight daughters and one son of five or six years old, had had to sell their house in Cheadle, Cheshire, and had bought the dress-making business in a desperate attempt to earn a living. We heard many details of how impoverished they were at that time. They had little opportunity for social life, apart from what the church provided, and even that might be precluded by having to work throughout the evening. Since they were numerous, however, they provided company for each other. Grannie had managed to keep most of her furniture – (her bed was a prize example) and the house was almost a working museum of the Victorian way of life. She was still alive at the time of my earlier visits; a rather formidable figure much revered by her daughters but somewhat feared by me. I sensed disapproval though without knowing why (probably because I still wet the bed). She didn't consider I could wash my own face properly and insisted on doing it for me but as she'd once had a stroke which half-paralysed her hand she jerked the flannel about my face in away which I found most unpleasant. In any case it was an important rule about children that one should not spoil them and she and her daughters took the greatest care not to spoil me, the more so as they one and all considered that Agnes (i.e. Mother) did.

They also clung to their gentility, a precious inheritance which could likewise be kept with a little effort and no expense. Grannie was undoubtedly a lady and took care that her daughters grew up the same. They in turn were much exercised that I should learn to be a gentleman. Madge in particular was continually correcting my manners and all of them were greatly concerned when, thanks to some of my Romford acquaintance, I seemed to be acquiring a cockney accent. They had little experience of boys, however, and their baby brother, seven years younger than Harriet, grew up to be a thoroughgoing ass who in due course made a disastrous marriage. (It seems more than likely that he'd been spoilt, being the only male in such a regiment of women.) 'Uncle John' (Bryson; there were two, one paternal the other maternal) was at the time in the Royal Flying Corps and seldom seen but as he had no use for children his absence didn't worry me.

The 'loo' in the Dingwall Road house was isolated at the end of a linoleum-covered stretch of landing which existed to serve it and had a window of many-coloured glass through which I used to stare at the neat front garden next door, fascinating because when you looked through the red parts at geraniums and salvias they looked white. It's 'throne' was more deserving of the name than most; a wide bench of polished wood with a hemi-spherical bowl of blue-patterned porcelain set in the middle and, at one side, a handle in a brass cup let into the bench. Flushing meant pulling up this handle thereby opening a circular hole in the bottom of the bowl and letting the water swirl in from the top. I found this rather intriguing and it seemed to me perfectly efficient but when they'd saved up enough money the Aunts had a more up-to-date one installed and clearly regarded it as a great improvement. I didn't share this view; the plug now hung from the cistern above and was beyond my reach so that I had to call for assistance.

The bathroom, which was next to the loo but approached from the other side of the staircase, had one narrow bath and was advanced enough to have a 'geyser'; a tall copper cylinder with a large gas ring at the bottom with a pilot-light on a hinge. To light it one turned this outwards, turned on the gas and applied a match, thus lighting the pilot-light, then turned it on its hinge inwards so that its flame jetted over the gas-ring which was then supposed to burst into flame. In practice it didn't do this at all readily and there was always an anxious moment while the gas poured out before igniting and sometimes an almighty bang when it finally did so. The bathroom's sash window had always to be open while this uncertain operation was in progress, even in the depth of winter, but in spite of this the smell of gas tended to hang about the room and sometimes invaded the house. The geyser was an Edwardian improvement but in spite of its uncertainties and its rather slow delivery of hot water it produced a bath more quickly and easily than when a servant had to carry cans of hot water upstairs from the kitchen.

Apart from gas, the chief bathroom smells were of TCP, of Kolynos toothpaste (also Edwardian, I fancy) and of Wright's Coal Tar Soap or 'curd' soap, these more hygenic odours being considered superior to scented perfumery. A more delicate fume associated with 'Croydon' was wafted at breakfast time: the smell of coffee, and more particularly of the methylated spirit burner which kept the 'coffee machine' bubbling. This was a tall and somewhat ornate pewter pot with long legs under which the burner was placed. The pot proper had a small tap at the bottom and a glass knob at the top through which periodic bubbles of hot black coffee could be seen. It stood in front of Grannie at the breakfast table – later in front of Aunt Pattie – and cups which needed filling were passed to her. When no more was likely to be needed she turned out the burner and the smell of burnt 'methylated' pervaded the room, a smell which betokened the end of breakfast and the sound of the seamstresses arriving, changing their boots in the back passage and going upstairs to the working-room.

Breakfast was a formal meal for which everyone assembled at table, having been summoned by the gong, usually rung by Harriet. Having seated ourselves we awaited grace said by Grannie, and later Pattie. No meal could begin before grace had been said. The menu always consisted of porridge, followed by kippers, or smoked haddock, or eggs and bacon, or sausages, followed by several slices of toast and marmalade.

Still, I believe breakfast for those on holiday or with leisure to eat such a large quantity of food, but Victorians who could afford it mostly ate far too much. Read about the kind of lunch that Dickens used to sit down to!

Part and parcel of every meal was Conversation which was at a higher level than mere chit-chat. Harriet, who was of a chirpy disposition, often had gossip from 'the Bank' to report but any contribution was addressed to the table at large and replied to in a similar manner, even when there were seven or eight people present. Breakfast was for the most part a family meal but at week-ends Harriet would sometimes invite a friend from the Bank, or Aunt Catherine and Alice would appear, both of them in the nursing profession, or of course Mother and Father. Politics were not barred as a subject of conversation, indeed they were quite a common one, though it tended to become acrimonious if Alice was present.

Alice, the next eldest after Mother, was matron of a large hospital run by the 'Metropolitan Asylums Board'. No doubt it was partly this position of authority that caused her to speak in a somewhat august and commanding manner but it also seemed to be innate. Both her manner and her accent seem to me in retrospect typically Victorian; I am reminded of her when I see certain Gilbertian heroines on the stage. Such a responsible post, especially in wartime, meant that her visits were rare but conversation tended to become acrimonious because, having studied in Wilhelmine Germany before the war, she was bitterly anti-German. She was also strongly Conservative reading the Morning Post while the rest of the family who were Liberals read the Daily News, or in Harriet's case, the Manchester Guardian. One such conversation ended with her saying to Mother 'Agnes, you're obsessed!'. What Mother was obsessed with, in fact what the word really meant, was lost on me, though I knew it couldn't be complimentary.

The table at which these conversations took place, and the dining-room chairs on which we sat, dated from the 1860s; the former oval, of massive mahogany, the latter also of mahogany, with open, oval-hooped backs, not very comfortable to sit back on but then at table one did not sit back; one sat up straight, and I was frequently commanded to do so. The huge sideboard, of walnut, was likewise massive and ornately carved but its drawers slid in and out with beautiful ease. Up to 1917 Grannie officiated but even after her death, when Pattie took the chair, the atmosphere remained almost identical, an atmosphere which I feel sure had continued unbroken since the 1880s. The table nearly always seemed to be well-populated and as there were originally eleven in the family this will have seemed normal. Cooking for large numbers was something the Victorians took for granted, though of course they also took servants for granted. The Aunts often spoke of 'Laura', their family servant 'before Father died', and quoted things she'd said. She came from Yorkshire, they told me, and it was thanks, vicariously, to Laura, that I first heard the expression 'You keep a dog and then bark yourself'. She'd clearly been very much part of the family. They were now able to afford a 'daily', a Mrs Potter, and sometimes even employed an errand-boy (was he, perhaps, Mrs Potter's son?) but in the evenings and at week-ends they did all the work themselves.

One characteristic sound in the house delighted me: the bells. At home we had electric bell-pushes in all rooms, operated by Leclanché cells (large square glass jars each containing a porous pot and a zinc rod in sal ammoniac) but at Croydon they still retained old-fashioned bells with clappers, each poised on a coiled ribbon of metal so that, when pulled, it wagged for several seconds with two claps for each wag. Within the house every room was provided with a bell-pull (to summon a servant) and at the front and back doors a brass handle in a brass cup – kept polished by the errand-boy when not otherwise engaged – was tugged briefly by callers. A big tug would produce a tremendous clangour and even some alarm as it sounded urgent enough to suggest 'a telegram!'. Telegrams were quite common (and remarkably speedy) but even so they tended to be associated with bad news. Telephones were coming in, however, and the Aunts, for all their old-fashionedness, were the first in the family to have one installed, chiefly because their wealthy clients would also have one and communications concerning dresses could be much more quickly and satisfactorily conveyed than via an errand-boy. The bells were ranged high up on the wall of the back passage, above a row of hooks where the seamstresses hung their coats, and in theory each had a separate note so that the initiated could tell the source of the ring. I never became initiated but enjoyed hearing them ring, indeed looked for opportunities to set one ringing. Electric bells, when they were later introduced, seemed to me rather a come-down.

Mention of the back passage brings back another 'Croydon' smell, viz. of the cellar just beside it; a dank, water-logged sort of smell that cellars tend to acquire in the course of time. The steps down to it were very steep but nevertheless much used. The cellar was the coolest place in the house (hence their commonness in the days before refrigerators) and so likely to be visited before and after every meal. It was illuminated by a tiny window beside the front-door steps and at the best of times was pretty dim. When night had fallen, or if greater illumination was required, one took a lighted wax taper. There was in fact a Fanny-by-gaslight gas jet but the Aunts had become fairly adept at finding their way about in the dark.

The coolness of the cellar was the more important as the kitchen, like most, had a 'kitchen range', i.e. a built-in iron cooking stove whose coal fire needed constant stoking. The sound of a shaken coalscuttle was another characteristic noise. There was usually a kettle simmering on the stove but when more direct heat was needed one removed a heavy circle of cast-iron immediately over the fire and the kettle or pan was placed over the hole. Cooking was in fact a chancy business since expertise in stoking and in the ways of the stove was needed to get the right heat, especially for the oven, but in this too the Aunts had become adept and all of them, especially Pattie, were excellent cooks. I find the recollection of it wafting another fume: a smell of sage, onions and oatmeal which I only smelt there. Was it perhaps a Scottish recipe for forcemeat?

Another device for keeping things cool, especially in summer, was the 'meat safe'; a small wooden cupboard with panels of perforated zinc in its sides and door, to let the air through, which was fixed to the north wall outside in the yard.

It was only partially successful and in hot weather was supplemented by putting such things as butter in a dish of cold water with wet muslin – known as 'butter muslin' – draped over it. The edges of the muslin soaked up the water which then evaporated, thus reducing the temperature underneath. This too was only partially successful and in summer butter could be pretty soft. It was made none the harder by the practice of serving it in little balls. A pair of 'butter pats' was kept in a jar of water (for coolness), one side of each lined with narrow grooves. One put a 'nut' of butter on the grooved side of one pat, rolled it against the grooved side of the other, thus producing a criss-cross pattern, and then put the resulting ball in a butter dish. Alternatively one could use a curious claw-like scraper which one drew along the surface of the butter so that it scraped up a thin, shell-shaped scroll. Butter dishes containing these little balls or scrolls were then placed about the table – so that everyone should have easy access to one – with delicate little forks or knives beside them, as well as dishes of various sorts of jam. Jam spoons and butter knives, or forks, were part of every household's stock-in-trade and were the sort of thing one could give as a present at Christmas. Bread was usually cut at table, on the breadboard, and handed to you thereon; it was considered most improper to pass it on the end of the bread-knife. You then helped yourself to a ball of butter which you first put on the side of your plate – it was also considered ill-bred to put it straight on the slice – and then spread it yourself. The bread was nearly always a little stale. New bread was supposed to be 'bad for you', although so much nicer, but this notion may originally have been due to economy. New bread was so popular that much more of it was consumed, especially by hungry children.

Butter was bought at the 'dairy' where the counters were lined with screened 'desks' behind which were solid 20lb lumps of butter. The serving girls – during the war it was usually girls – armed with rather larger pats than the domestic ones, would hack out a lump of approximately the size you wanted – it could be two pounds if you had large numbers at home – pound it vigorously into a brick shape, lay a piece of grease-proof paper on the scales, clash the appropriate brass weight into the other half, place the brick on the paper, add or subtract bits of butter until the scales broke even, remove it from the scales, pat it into a final brick shape and then fold it into the paper by hand. This was not the end. It was then placed in brown grease-proof paper, wrapped into a parcel and finally tied with string, with a special loop of string for you to put your finger through to carry it. Around 1917 the price rose to *two shillings a pound*! a price that aroused horror and induced many people to buy it by the half-pound or else switch to margarine. Pictures of 'Dairyland' on the front of the desks with their accompanying legends made it clear that Maypole butter came from Congleton in Cheshire. The wartime shortage will have been mainly due to labour shortage. When milking was done by hand dairying must have been pretty labour-intensive. There were 'landgirls' during that war but girls were much in demand for making munitions.

Nearly everything was labour-intensive. Vacuum cleaners existed but the suction was produced by a hand pump, the bellows being fixed to a small floorboard on which one stood to keep it firm while wagging the handle back and forth with one hand and moving the pipe, with its long narrow slit of a pick-up, across the carpet with the other. This was not only exhausting (and far less efficient than electric suction) but one could only get at the little bit of carpet within one's immediate reach. That done, one had to move the whole contraption on to the next bit of carpet, and so on. If two people did the job it was very much quicker and I was often deputed to pump the bellows – when my weight was sufficient to hold them in position and even then I could easily shake myself off the floorboard. Carpets, at the annual spring-cleaning, had to be scrubbed by hand which meant spending long periods on one's knees. Mats and small carpets were hauled out into the garden and hung on the clothes line to be beaten. 'Carpet beaters' were made of flexible wicker-work woven into a sort of long-handled racket, and wielding them was a lot more exhausting than it looked but at least you had the satisfaction of seeing the dust come out.

Despite the labour, however, the Aunts were indefatigable cleaners. A normal sound when one woke up in the morning was of Harriet brushing down the staircase with a dustpan and brush, her hair covered with a cloth bathing-cap to keep the dust out, or polishing the shiny linoleum floors with a mop – all this before breakfast (it might explain their large breakfasts). She often sang as she worked, Gilbert and Sullivan as likely as not. A sunny morning would evoke 'Brightly dawns our wedding day' or 'The flowers that bloom in the spring, tra-la' (Gilbert and Sullivan around the turn of the century must have been as all-pervading as coal smoke, if not more so). It was in any case a social convention that everyone should 'sing', whether they had a voice or not, and everyone who could afford it had a piano. When invited to someone's house one took one's music, often hoping that someone there would be available to play the accompaniment. Skill at the piano was much in demand and I was sent to have music lessons from the age of six, largely so that I should be available to play accompaniments with the minimum delay.

The piano at Dingwall Road, a battle-scarred war-horse that had been at the service of the eight sisters, was a Collard & Collard and had panels of walnut 'fretwork' over pleated green silk with a pair of brass candlesticks on each side. I was conscious that its tone was inferior to our piano at Romford but at least they kept it tuned and as my music lessons involved 'practising' they kept me up to mark in that, as well as getting me to study some of the easier accompaniments to their songs. This I rather enjoyed as it allowed me to feel grown up and encouragement stimulated progress. I couldn't stretch an octave but soon learnt that one of the two notes would do. One song which Madge and Harriet sang as a duet was the 'Barcarolle' from Offenbach's 'Tales of Hoffmann', and a solo of Harriet's, 'She is far from the land' moved me almost to tears. Other more deserving songs came from a volume of 'Tchaikowsky's Songs' bound in crimson leather and with gilt edgings, in particular 'To the Forest' and 'Fifinella'. To hear them again would bring back that Croydon drawing-room alive in its zeitgeist, especially Harriet's light soprano voice. I find both words and music of a 'light ballad' called 'The Little Damozel' coming along with them.

At home in Romford, Sunday afternoon meant Sunday School but at Croydon it meant 'a walk', usually in the direction of 'the Surrey hills' around Shirley and Addington. One seldom had to go far to reach quiet, unpolluted countryside. Until the 1920s even Purley was not much more than a slender accretion of ribbon-building along the railway and the Brighton main road. 'Purley Way' didn't come into existence as the Croydon by-pass until the 1920s and at that time felt as a new motorway does now. My brother-in-law once did *fifty miles an hour*! along it in his Morris Hotchkiss – admittedly going downhill. A favourite place for a picnic, fairly close by, was Croham Hurst and it was quite a secluded spot. They usually took a book for reading aloud (an old pre-radio pastime) and as Pattie was deaf she was the obvious candidate for doing the reading, even when walking along, supported on each side by Madge and Harriet who thus spared her the necessity of looking where she was going. The books read were usually by Mrs Molesworth. One was called *Hetty Gray* and another *Carrots* which referred to a boy with red hair, 'the baby of the family'; not only the youngest but 'very much the youngest' (casting a certain light, I now see, on that little brother of theirs who grew up to be my wicked uncle). Mrs Molesworth was chosen because they already had her books and she was considered 'suitable for children' (but also, I fancy, for nostalgtic associations with their own childhood and the time 'before Father died').

The return from the walk, and for me the most exciting part of it, took us along a path beside the railway just south of East Croydon station. With any luck one might see one of the LBSC expresses on its way to or from Worthing, Newhaven or Chichester tearing past (probably at about 50mph) drawn by a Baltic 4-6-4T or a 'Marsh' Atlantic. On the other side of the tracks towards Park Lane (where the Fairfield Hall now stands) was a coal-cum-shunting yard and beyond it, on the other side of Park Lane, were the Katherine Street Gardens. I was much intrigued to learn from Madge one day that when they'd first came to live in Croydon this garden site had been occupied by 'Croydon Central Station', a terminus, and that East Croydon had then boasted a mere couple of wooden platforms. The two were only a few hundred yards apart but in the early days, Madge said, people regarded suburban trains as something like tram services and no one fussed about how often a train started and stopped.

One day – it will have been after the war – I was suprised to see a train pull into East Croydon station with Midland (LMS?) coaches mixed up with LBSC ones, complete with dining-car, and mentioned the fact when I returned to Dingwall Road. Madge then told me this was the 'Sunny South Express', a through train between south coast resorts and Manchester and Liverpool. Further enquiry revealed that, northwards from Croydon, it stopped at Clapham Junction and there branched onto the 'West London Line' which took it through 'Battersea', 'Chelsea & Fulham', 'Addison Road' and finally Willesden Junction where it joined the North-Western main line. One of the nuisances of north-south travel was getting across London whose many termini were widely separated. Even Londoners who lived near Chelsea, Fulham etc were glad to be spared the trouble and expense of going first to Euston or Victoria; it will have more than compensated for the many starts and stops.

Railways in their prime, above all in the 1930s, were the optimum form of travel and it is hardly surprising if so many look back on them with affection. You could sit comfortably in a spacious compartment, with plenty of knee-room, and read a book, or look out of the window, or chat to fellow-passengers, while the driving was left to professionals. Come mealtime, on a good train, you could walk up the corridor to the dining-car and get an excellent meal, with wine, while still enjoying all three. Coaches and aircraft are far more cramped. Private cars are all very convenient but in relation to the number of people transported are grossly extravagant with both fuel and land, and have done far greater damage to the environment in the way of motorways, car parks, and general restlessness, quite apart from accidents. Railway accidents are rare; road crashes a daily occurrence. Railways, since they could face neither steep gradients nor sharp curves, had to worm and burrow their way through the countryside, and even a double-track line takes up less room than the average main road. It was their turning up in unexpected places that constituted a large part of their magic. Here, suddenly, on a wet Thursday afternoon beyond a bed of nettles, white letters on a black background formed the words 'Midland Railways'; a short slope led to the station and in due course a red magic carpet – the fastest thing on earth! – was rolled out before you and in what seemed no time transported you to another place that had formerly seemed not only remote but almost inaccessible. Places, in the early twentieth century, were far more remote from one another than they have since become, thanks to cars, and as a result had a quietness and a savour which they have since lost. I shall never forget the first time I used the Great Western Railway to visit 'Cousin Alice' in Trowbridge. I seemed to be in a different country but I shall reserve the pleasure of writing about it for a later chapter.

Music

An evangelistic 'chorus' in which I was once required to join had the refrain:

> Count your blessings. Count them one by one,
> And it will surprise you what the Lord has done.

Balance sheets comparing the past with the present can sometimes surprise one with what the Lord has done on the credit side; people who, in the 1980s, buy some beautiful eighteenth-century house are unlikely to live in it before making radical improvement to the bathroom and kitchen and one feels little doubt that ancestral ghosts would approve. If I concede one somewhat qualified cheer for the car I can give a hearty one for the gramophone and an even heartier third for what Lord Reith and his BBC have done. These have so transformed the musical scene in this country as to make the Victorians and the Edwardians seem musically illiterate in retrospect. Apart from the piano, and to a lesser extent the organ, few people then learnt an instrument – in England; Germany was another matter – and many who could have afforded it and had the leisure nevertheless failed to take one up. By and large they were a pretty philistine lot; one has only to look at the programmes of the earliest Proms to see their level of taste. Those seriously interested in music, even professors of music in academies and colleges, and other similarly placed, in order to extend their musical knowledge often had to resort to the piano duet and the chances were that they'd never heard proper performances of works which are now considered standard repertory. They might go for miles to hear an orchestra or a string quartet but one concert can only include a few works, and many a supposed 'expert' probably only knew by hearsay, if that, of such masterpieces as Mozart's string quintets. For those who couldn't afford a piano, however, or for many who could, there was another way in, namely choirs, and that way was usually via the church.

Madge sang contralto in the choir of the South Croydon Congregational curch and she, and later Harriet for a while, graduated from this to the Croydon Philharmonic Choir. They were, in fact, seriously interested in music and would have been far more skilled and knowledgeable about it if their father's early death hadn't deprived them of the time and money to study it. He, according to Mother, played the violin 'divinely' and although I knew he'd been canonised posthumously, the fact that he played it at all was a strong point in his favour. Both she and Father believed in starting children young and even when I started piano lessons aged six I already knew the names of the notes, having picked them up from Pen, though I used to think, regretfully, that I'd never be able to catch up with her as she'd always be three and a half years older and so always ahead of me.

The lessons were with a Miss Barber, a quiet modest woman who took her work and her pupils seriously. Her method of putting musical instruction across was called 'the Curwen method' and although it meant knowing the names of the note values – semibrieve, minim, crotchet, quaver, etc. – it also provided shorthand names which could be sung to the speed of the music. A crotchet was 'Ta' and was extended through further beats by 'ah'; a minim was therefore 'Ta–ah' and a semibrieve 'Ta–ah–ah–ah'. A quaver was 'tay', two quavers 'ta–tay', and four semi-quavers 'Tafa–taffy'. Her blackboard was ruled with painted staves and a given exercise was in five parts:

1 Miss Barber announced the time-signature which the pupil then had to write on the board while she stood with her back to the piano with the fingers of her left hand poised over a note. The pupil then turned and faced her.

2 Consisted in beating 'a bar for nothing' by both parties with the pupil reciting 'One · two · three · four' (or whatever).
3 Beating continued while she tapped a phrase on one note.
4 The pupil, still beating, had to chant the phrase, e.g. 'Ta · ah–tay · tafa–taffy · ta'.
5 The pupil then turned and wrote the notes on the blackboard:

It had the virtue of getting one used to writing music down. Once one could be trusted to get the values right and ensure that the bar added up to four crochets – or whatever – one got on to more advanced exercises: she announced the key as well and instead of simple note values one had little snippets of tune to be written down in the correct lines and spaces (the opening bars of 'God save the King' are indelibly engraved on my mind, thanks to this). Learning the various keys meant going to the piano where attention was given to scales and arpeggios, with due attention to fingering, and we were inducted into the mysteries of major and minor scales, but it was above all the habit of writing music down which paved the way for musical literacy and ability to sight-read. Mr Curwen had imaginatively provided duets in his book, the lower part for the pupil to play – beginning in very simple notes in octaves, one note for each hand – while Miss Barber played a much more complicated upper part, thus making one feel that one was almost playing, certainly contributing to, a much more advanced and complex piece. That, however, only happened at the lesson. For home practice we had Walter Carroll's 'Scenes on the Farm', very simple pieces but surprisingly effective (and still indeliby engraved; I recently discovered that 'The little brook' and 'On the lake' were still at my finger's ends, the latter bringing alive our Edwardian drawing-room on a sad autumn morning in 1916. Its melancholy was part of its charm, further enhanced by the recollection of Bassenthwaite Lake where I'd been for the previous summer holiday).

Mother can hardly have been dissatisfied with Miss Barber but one day she was told (by Mrs Gibson of whom more anon) of a certain Miss Snell who was supposed to be a great one for getting children through their exams, and generally cracking up the latter's virtues, one of which was that she came to the house – on her bicycle. Mother allowed herself to be persuaded and told me she was switching to a new teacher though I gave little thought to what she might have told Miss Barber and as a result, at my last lesson, let the cat out of the bag. At the end of it she gave me a rather reproachful 'I hope you get on all right with your new teacher' and when I reported this to Mother she was very upset. I duly felt guilty about hurting Miss Barber's feelings and wondered what Mother had said to her. It wasn't like Mother to tell diplomatic lies – or not on any serious scale. She'd have done better to take me into her confidence about what she had said, even if it meant making me part to some diplomatic 'evasion'. I'd gladly have cooperated in sparing Miss Barber's feelings and would have learnt something about tact and diplomacy in the process.

Miss Snell was a very different kettle of fish. Whereas Miss Barber had been slim, serious and rather restrained, Miss Snell was buxom, very forthright, and by comparison almost a bully. Soon after the lessons started she got married and thereafter gave herself the professional name of Madame Snell so that people would realise that they were still dealing with the same person. Before long she became even more buxom by becoming pregnant but until a very late stage she continued to ride over from Wanstead on her bicycle. I was conscious of her fatness as I sat beside her at the piano but being ignorant of the facts of life I'd no idea of the reason, nor did it occur to me that her condition might make her more easily exasperated. She just seemed easily exasperated and would scrawl imperious instructions on my pieces, sometimes, in extreme cases, in *blue pencil* so that they couldn't be rubbed out and *the examiner would see them*! One of my books dating from that time still has *'Count aloud, Bryson'* scrawled across one of its pages in bold Madame Snell handwriting.

She was undoubtedly thorough and allowed nothing that was in the least slipshod to pass. Major and minor scales and arpeggios were hammered at unmercifully with the greatest attention to correct fingering but part of her exasperation was that I didn't practice enough, and this was undeniable. Admittedly practising had to be fitted in with homework from school but I didn't appreciate how far practising is the secret of playing well. I did, however, sometimes wish that she'd be less imperious and more encouraging. I would often declare great enthusiasm for a given piece but it was not in her nature to share enthusiasms, or not with the likes of me – and not with her matrimonial preoccupations. Her main concern was to look out for faults and pounce on them and she evidently felt that this was her real job, the job of all good teachers in fact. Very occasionally she would order me out of my seat, shift her weighty bulk into it and enrapture me with a demonstration. To see a piece I'd been struggling with given a polished performance was an eye-opener into the art of the possible.

In due course I sat for the Lower Division exam, which meant going up to London, one fine day in high summer, to the Royal College of Music behind the Albert Hall. I was much over-awed and the examiner, a man, seemed bored and did nothing to put me at my ease so that my nervousness increased. Moreover, thanks to the weather, all the windows in the huge building were wide open and out of every one came the sounds of singing, playing the piano, the violin and various other instruments, thus producing a distracting jangle of noise. When, a few weeks later, the results came out I learnt that I'd failed by seven marks, my weakest subject being 'Ear-training', a thing I was supposed to be good at. Ear-training tests meant that the examiner played a chord and one was required to sing the lowest or the middle note of it, or he played a note and one had to sing a fifth (or whatever) higher or lower, etc. but that jangle of noise drove all attempts at concentration out of my head. I didn't dare mention it to the examiner but I did explain to Madame Snell. She didn't say much. Maybe she saw my point but she probably felt that my failure reflected on her.

Nevertheless thanks to her efforts and Miss Barber's 'Music' already had a life of its own independently of lessons. One bit of independent activity arose from the fact that the Croydon Philharmonic, with Madge in the choir, were due to give a performance of 'Hiawatha's Wedding Feast' in the Baths Hall, and as Mother had a copy of the vocal score I got it out, played what I could as best I could, and took it to the concert with me when the great night arrived. This was an eye-opener into what an orchestra could do. At the piano I'd been concerned with notes and hadn't given a thought to what instruments would play them so that I was electrified when the by-now-familiar opening fanfare was proclaimed by trumpet and flute, and even more so when the slow, 'jungle' rhythm which followed it: 'Ta–ah · Ta · Ta' on reiterated fifths in the left hand here brought the drums into service with almost sinister effect. As for the 'Dance of Pau-Puk-Keewis', I'd found it unplayable on the piano, yet now the orchestra reeled off the 'terribly difficult' notes with wild abandon and the utmost ease. By that time I was completely carried away and had never followed anything with such intense interest for so long (except Peter Pan a few years before). It seemed marvellously snug round the camp fire with the great dark forest behind; perfectly right and proper that all their belts should be made of 'wampum' – whatever that might be – and that they should feast on 'pemmican' and 'the wild rice of the river'.

After the performance I listened to a conversation between Madge and Harriet about Colerdige-Taylor and was amazed to learn that he was 'coloured' and lived in Croydon. Madge said he'd had something to do with the Presbyterian church, which was just near the end of Dingwall Road. Harriet, who'd been reading the programme notes, came across with the information that Elgar had promoted his career, and Elgar's name was familiar to me as his 'Salut d'Amour' was one of my pieces. A thing I didn't appreciate was how refreshing 'Hiawatha' must have seemed to choirs in 1898 (when it first appeared) after years of Stainer's 'Crucifixion', but for me it had been more than refreshing; it had been a revelation. I'd caught a glimpse of something called 'orchestration'.

Thanks to scores, Western music has become an immense body of knowledge – and 'knowledge' seems the only appropriate word for it. Admittedly it is only expressible in its own terms; attempts to describe it in words, pictures or other forms are never more than the roughest and most inadequate approximations, but within those terms it transcends language and speaks directly to the mind, penetrating to the most secret corners of the cortex. Smells can do the same but can't be organised in the same way; Scriabin's attempt to write a smell symphony merely proved the point. Both can bring the past back alive but when smells do so it's a matter of chance; with music it has been 'composed' and the depth and diversity of experience that can be caught in its net is astonishing. A few years ago I happened across a copy of Tchaikowsky's 'Album for the Young' of which several pieces had been the victims of my youthful endeavours under Madame Snell, one of them called 'The New Doll'. Playing it again after a lapse of some six decades I suddenly found a whole world of the past coming alive along with it: not only my appreciation of Tchaikowsky's appreciation of a little Russian girl's delight in her new doll; not only reminders of what I'd found technically difficult about it, but a sudden vision of seventy years ago: our Edwardian drawing-room with its Strohmenger piano and its coal fire on a winter's day; Czarist Russia, Lenin/Trotsky's Russia, all that I'd heard or read and sometimes forgotten about 'Russia' was suddenly retrieved alive by the simple process of playing a few simple notes on the piano. Music clearly by-passes thought processes and gets nearer the root of the human psyche than any other of Man's discoveries. If we are going to attempt to communicate with possible planets in other solar systems, music is clearly the most promising language in which to do so. Like mathematics, it is in tune with the Infinite.

I'm therefore not really suprised to find that there is an undercurrent of music – of the most diverse sorts – throughout this book. Like most others, I can measure out my life with popular tunes, but away from the eternal flow of 'pop', with its period reminders, there have been moments when passages – usually quite short passages – of more serious music have moved me to the depths of my being without my being able to say why, or what it was 'about', and this is a fairly common experience. At the moment of being moved one ceases to be aware of sounds, as such, and receives a communication from 'elsewhere'. From the composer, yes, but where did he – that genius – get if from?

Miss Jones's

With hindsight I can see that Mother will have switched from Miss Newman's to Miss Jones's because the latter was 'a lady' and had a nicer class of pupil, though this was not the sort of thing she would have mentioned to us. The fact that the pupils were nearly all girls would not have seemed to her in any way an objection; probably rather the reverse. She and her sisters, with no brothers except a baby one and for much of their lives no father, knew little of the male sex at first hand and rather disapproved of what they did know; boys were 'rough' and much naughtier than girls. Moreover their Feminist leanings had probably encouraged a feeling that women, if not actually superior, were more civilized. Of the fourteen or so pupils at Miss Jones's during the three years I went there, only two of us were boys except for a term or two when Dick Dendy made a third. Miss Jones may well have shared these Feminist leanings. She certainly believed that boys should learn to make themselves useful and among other accomplishments, taught us how to sew on buttons. I docilely allowed myself to be taught – and to be frank have never regretted the know-how – but Pat Conly, the other boy, made a lamentable hash of his. His father was a red-headed Irishman who no doubt scoffed at such effeminate occupations and Pat probably took his cue from this.

Not that our education was chiefly concerned with such activities; they were a tiny part of it. Much higher priority was 'French without Tears' on which we were at once launched: '*Charles a un canif . . . Robert prend son canif . . . Charles pleure*'. It seemed to me stupid to call the book 'French without Tears' and then, in the very first exercise, have Charles shed tears, though on one occasion, doing my homework, I shed tears myself at the difficulty of it and threw the book on the floor. Miss Jones was something of a Francophile, quite apart from patriotic sentiments, and had made frequent visits to France before the war. She gave us a positive crash course in French and since the ice had already been broken for me by 'Mademoiselle' at Miss Newman's I made fairly rapid progress, indeed by the age of eight was already having 'Conversation' classes. A few of us, by special arrangement with our parents, stayed late twice a week for 'Extra French' and sat round Miss Jones's little dining-room table attempting to think up things to say, much prompted by her. We were far from fluent but the effort of articulating it, helped on by the ocassional success with a word or phrase, provided at least the entrée to greater fluency as well as familiarising us with common or garden words. One of her devices was to get us to say what we'd had for our meals so that we were soon familiar with *pommes, pommes de terre, chou, chou-fleur,* choux de Bruxelles, etc. and with the various condiments: *du sel, du poivre, et du vinaigre.* The word *vinaigre* was particularly stamped on my mind as one of the girls, Enid Channon, had discovered that Miss Jones didn't like vinegar and therefore always made a point of saying she'd had some, whereupon Miss Jones gave a facetious shudder.

This kind of jibe was typical of Enid who provided my first acquaintance with the Ugly Duckling mentality. Not only did she have a spotty skin, and wore metal-rimmed glasses, but she had an embittered disposition. She enjoyed recounting other people's – especially Miss Jones's – misfortunes, or being derisive, or scoring little triumphs of one-up-manship. On one occasion, as a week-end task, we had to learn two verses from the New Testament, the choice being left to us, and then, on Monday, give chapter and verse and recite them. It was typical of Enid that she chose Luke, 17:32 'Remember Lot's wife', and John, 11:35 'Jesus wept', crowning this briefest possible of recitations with a smug grin as much as to say 'Aren't I clever!'. She had a younger sister, Margaret, a spoilt girl who was reported as being 'Daddy's favourite' and was certainly prettier, but I disliked her less than I disliked Enid.

'Scripture' was of course part of the curriculum and one of my first school books, much more beautifully bound than the rest, was 'Holy Bible'. Reading from the Bible, though part of a Scripture lesson, also did service as Reading Practice. Most of us could read, more or less, by the time we went there but practice was obviously needed. It could also be practised by attaching it to History. We had 'Little Arthur's England' and took it in turns to read a sentence or two from that so that one might hear, say, Margaret Channon, who was less practised than most, struggling with 'They cut off his head in such a cruel way that his cries and shrieks were heard all over the castle'. This referred to Edward II's end in Berkeley Castle and I imagined them doing it with a blunt kitchen knife. Once through with Little Arthur we graduated to more detailed history with a series by 'Ed. J.S. Lay' and I came in for the Stuart period with more, if less cruel, cutting off of heads, an activity which horrified me enough to be the subject of at least two nightmares. It was something of a relief that King Charles's head was cut off 'at one blow'.

Miss Jones was a great believer in learning by heart and for homework we had to memorise the dates of the Stuart kings and then recite them when back at school, as a result of which I learnt the dates of the Norman kings as well through hearing Pen memorise them at home (and know them still). Multiplication Tables were included in this basic programming, as were Troy Weight, Avoirdupois Weight, Long Measure, Dry Measure, et al. 'Hearing our tables' was a daily routine. Our Table Book – Wightman's – contained other information which we didn't have to learn by heart but stuck in spite of it, e.g. that the American Dollar was worth 4s 2d., nearly five dollars to the pound sterling.

Not all our lessons were so pragmatic. Poetry was an important subject and again one for memorisation, in fact a poem which Pen had to learn by heart at home shortly before I went there, but was aware that I was due to go, had formed a sort of magic spell whose incantation pre-figured 'Miss Jones's':

> I come from haunts of coot and hern,
> I make a sudden sally,
> And sparkle out among the fern
> To bicker down a valley . . .
>
> I chatter, chatter as I flow
> To join the brimming river;
> For men may come and men may go,
> But I go on for ever.

Part of its magic was its use of unknown words; 'haunts of coot and hern' was for me a piece of abracadabra; I'd no idea what it really meant. Sometimes I plucked up courage to ask what a new word meant but more often I kept quite about my ignorance and found out by further listening though it was a good many years before I discovered that a coot was a bird and still more before 'hern' was identified as a 'heron'. Hern seemed to have more wizardly possibilities. 'Sally' I knew only as a girl's name though not that of any girl I knew; it was thanks to 'Sally in our Alley', a song in the Scottish Student's songbook. 'Bicker' was familiar at home – Aunt Elsie had once commanded us to 'stop bickering' – but it was not an activity I expected a brook to be accused of. A different sort of magic was evoked by 'here and there a grayling'. Thanks to my butterfly book I knew (or thought I knew) what a grayling was, though I'd never seen a live specimen, and I imagined one flying over the brook.

Despite mystifications, however, I understood the basic theme of the poem very well. I even managed to savour the imagery and onomatopoeia of 'babble over pebbles' but above all I appreciated the sense of time and eternity conjured up by:

> Men may come and men may go,
> But I go on for ever.

Behind it all lay the awareness that Pen, three-and-a-half years older than I, was learning it, that it was part of a more grown-up world I was shortly to move into, (and I'm surprised how the spell can be re-cast when I hear 'The Brook' quoted, or even when I read it; it brings back the past in the same way as music). When in due course I attended the school I was soon put to work memorising poems myself and at the words:

> So here hath been dawning
> Another blue day.
> Think, wilt thou let it
> Slip useless away?

I can at once smell the cedar-wood smell of sharpened pencils and see our pencil-boxes with their long sliding tops. My mind was arrested by the concept of a blue day, in fact words were daily tending to arrest. In our spelling lessons, for which we all had carboard letters and had to set out on our desks words spoken by Miss Jones, we one day had the word SCOTCH. This was familiar enough; it applied to my ancestors, but it suddenly seemed to me an extraordinary word. I said it to myself over and over again and each time it seemed more extraordinary. Then the fit passed and it became ordinary again.

I first attended the school at the beginning of the summer term (of 1917) and before long there came what seemed to me a very blue day; a glorious June morning with a gentle breeze. As it was warm Miss Jones suggested we might open the windows wider and when a breeze blew in from the hayfields across Butts Lane and lifted the curtains Freda Barrington – a very pretty girl and my favourite – described it as 'heavenly'. This too was an arresting word which it would never have occured to me to use, having previously known it only in connection with 'our heavenly Father', and my mind registered the use of it as sophisticated, perhaps even fashionable in Freda's circles. Freda, with her fair curly hair and lively good-natured disposition, was my first love and had a kind of aura. I imagined her living in 'beautiful' surroundings with lots of other beautiful people though I should have been quite unable to supply details of what that beauty consisted in. In the event – though it was a few years later – Pen and I were invited to tea at the Barringtons and the details were filled in; they had a tennis-court in their garden and were the first people we ever met to have a 'wireless set', then the very latest thing; a 'crystal set' with a 'cat's whisker' which we were allowed to operate, with earphones on our heads.

There was another Freda in the school, Freda Wilson, the oldest girl there. She, and May Chipperfield – all these names are engraved on my mind – had reached the hoary age of *fourteen*! For the big girls there was another poetry book with rather more grown-up poetry, and more than mere learning by heart was required of them; they had to 'recite' it to the entire class. If I still know most of Kipling's 'Our England is a garden' by heart it's because Pen had to commit it to memory at home. Another poem was W.E. Henley's 'England, my England'. Either May or Freda Wilson might hold the floor with this and they gave it the full treatment while we listened in reverent silence and felt patriotic. 'Recitation' was another (pre-radio) pursuit suitable for social occasions, particularly for those without musical skills, but I became aware that, just as many people 'sang' who hadn't got a voice, so did many 'recite' without any capacity for words and their declamation. Enid's recitations made this abundantly clear:

> You'll *find* the *tool* and *potting sheds*
> Which *are* the *heart* of *all*.

It was embarrassing to have to listen to her inexorable bumpety-bump.

Nevertheless, especially with the better reciters, words could still impinge their unexpectedness. Henley's poem contained the lines:

> With your glorious eyes austere,
> As the Lord were walking near

> Whispering terrible things, and dear
> To that song on your bugles blown.

and it was the word 'terrible' that impinged. Surely the Lord had no business to whisper *terrible* things? Much the same applied to Kipling's:

> God of our fathers, known of old,
> Lord of our far-flung battle-line,
> Beneath whose awful hand we hold
> Dominion over palm and pine.

How could God's hand be *awful*?

Quite a different aspect of words was studied under Grammar and Parsing; we learnt about Nouns, Adjectives, Verbs, Adverbs and the rest. 'A noun is a name.' 'A Proper Noun will have a capital letter.' I found Conjunctions particularly hard to identify, in fact Grammar was a very difficult subject though it was perhaps helped by having to study French. One exercise, concerning Suffixes, was entitled 'Adding -hood': man- manhood, boy- boyhood, etc. and at the end one was required to think up a few examples oneself. Once, overlooking Pen's exercise book, I saw that she'd thought up 'mackintosh- mackintosh-hood' and that Miss Jones had ringed it round in red pencil.

Geography, too, was diligently studied and lessons ended with verbal interrogations: 'How do we know that the world is round? A. Because men have sailed round it.' 'What is an isthmus? A. A narrow neck of land joining two larger pieces.' 'What's the capital of Switzerland? A. Bern on the Aar'; 'What's the capital of Germany? A. Berlin on the Spree' and sometimes Miss Jones, only half in joke, would end up with 'What's the capital of the world?' to which the answer, chorussed out by the entire class, was 'London on the Thames'. All this information is still there, retrievable when required, though some of it is now out of date; Norway's capital is no longer called Christiania, nor Russia's Petrograd, and few of the world's inhabitants would now regard London as its capital but the Imperialist age around us was a good deal enhanced by the war.

Handwriting, of course, was a 'must' and here I was caught between two schools. At Miss Newman's we'd been given 'pothooks and hangers', i.e. copperplate, but in this Miss Jones was 'modern' and continually commanding us to write 'round and upright'. Things were further complicated when I went to the City of London School where it was back to copperplate again.

The most enjoyable lesson of the week was Painting. We took our own paintboxes, the inkwells on our desks were replaced by little pots of water, and we spent the whole morning at it. The first part was devoted to 'brush strokes'; special 'Painting Books' were divided into sections of about an inch square, and we had to take a 'full-but-not-too-full' brushful of paint and lay a carrot-shaped blob obliquely across a square from corner to corner. In a really good one the point of the carrot was very pointed and widened evenly to the blunt end which was nicely rounded and which, thanks to the slope of the desk, dried a deeper colour. Miss Jones was very insistent that we should not have our colours too dry, and particularly liked the exploitation of little pools of deeper colour which could result if one was skilful enough. Once, in the course of her progress round the class to see how we'd been getting on, she startled and half-embarrassed me by kissing me on the cheek for a couple of unusually successful blobs.

After the blobbing we could paint something from our imaginations. Trees were a popular – though 'very difficult' – choice, and she was constantly repeating 'Always put a little Burnt Sienna with your greens', advice which astounded me when I first heard it as I'd always been confident that for Green one mixed Prussian Blue with Gamboge. Those whose imaginations weren't working well could bring a leaf or a flower, picked on the way to school, and paint that. May Chipperfield's lifelike representations of ivy leaves were much admired. At the end of each term was a special exhibition for parents to come and see and I was surprised on one occasion to find that one of my leaves had been chosen for exhibition. It had blobbed successfully – largely by luck – with the Burnt Sienna half-separated from the blue and yellow. To be among the few singled out in this way made me respect her disapproval of Chinese White. According to her the whitest thing you could have was the paper itself and you could enhance its whiteness by the colours you put round it.

Her kissing me, however, was exceptional and not at all typical; for the most part she was strict and sometimes very censorious. Once May brought a 'Holiday picture', i.e. one she'd done during the holidays, of a bridge over a river which we all thought marvellous but it was somehow bruited perhaps her sister Joy had sneaked that she'd 'copied it' and this was Mortal Sin. May must have admitted to the crime as Miss Jones ceremoniously tore the picture up before the entire class and poor May was in disgrace – and her lovely picture in tatters.

Worse punishment could be in store for other offences, particularly for Pat and me – 'the boys'. She once caned me across the palm of my hand with a knitting needle though I never knew exactly for what crime and felt it to be very unjust. Whether the girls were thus punished I never heard as it was not done in public; one had to 'stay behind after school', sinister words which produced dread, but on the face of it corporal punishment was reserved for boys. There was one occasion when Pat and I were on the mat because the mother of one of the girls, Ruth Brewitt, had written her a letter complaining that we'd tormented her daughter on the way home. We had in fact ragged her a little but nothing worse. Ruth, however, was an only child and we regarded her as 'spoilt'. All those who'd been in the homeward party – except Ruth – had to 'stay behind' and were then interrogated on what exactly had taken place, Enid being the chief spokesman as she was the eldest. Enid was unable to produce any very damning evidence against us but said that, at one point, we'd called Ruth 'a little lion' and for a moment I was wildly alarmed as we had in fact called her 'a little liar' and 'liar' was a word I'd been forbidden to use by Father. Fortunately we'd shouted it from far enough away for Enid to mishear – it was a parting shot – and Miss Jones merely remarked that it seemed 'a funny name to call her'; (Ruth was more like a mouse). She gave us a brief lecture on home-going behaviour and then dismissed us.

This incident was highly instructive although no punishment ensued. I was aware that Enid, although giving evidence as a seemingly detached and virtuous witness, had in fact half-joined in the ragging – which was right up her street – though she made no admission of it. I also knew that girls were just as capable of ragging as boys. There'd been an early home-going occasion when May, who was twice my size, had seized my cap and hung it on the branch of a tree where I couldn't reach it and then run away. I cried with frustration and was acutely conscious of their collective derision but even if I'd mentioned the fact when I got home I felt sure that Mother would never have written a letter of complaint about it to Miss Jones and I sensed that the latter, although apparently administering stern justice on behalf of Mrs Brewitt, didn't like mothers who wrote letters of complaint and so was not entirely on her side; that there could be cracks in the conspiracy of Grown-ups v. Children. Some grown-ups, it appeared, were not all as Good as I'd tended to believe.

Looking back on the three years I spent at Miss Jones's I find myself full of admiration at the amount of useful knowledge she managed to pack into them and get remembered, especially as we only attended in the mornings. This was partly because she was an educated woman herself, partly because I was at a receptive age when nearly everything gets remembered, and perhaps above all because we were few in number. A class of fourteen gets a good deal more individual attention than one of thirty, and for much of the time half of us would be given a written task while the other half was being personally supervised. Moreover she never talked down to children; she treated us as intelligent human beings so that we responded as such. And there were few teachable activities she didn't tackle. I haven't mentioned the Singing Class for which we repaired downstairs to her drawing-room as a break from more brain-stretching occupations. Some of the songs were rather Victorian; I particularly recall a graveyardy nostalgic one called 'Those Evening Bells' but recall it chiefly because I learnt to sing 'seconds' in it, i.e. contralto; and can sing it still. In most respects she was 'modern', as with handwriting, and come Christmas she introduced us to traditional carols such as 'The moon shines bright' and 'The holly and the ivy', then little known but recently introduced as part of the Cecil Sharp folk revival. Thanks to them I sensed a much older England associated with the Golden Lion at Romford. For her time she was clearly pretty alert to what was happening in the arts.

At some point in 1919, or early 1920, I had to go up to London with Father for an interview for the City of London School. It was a brief one in the study of the headmaster, Dr Arthur Chilton, D.D. Father warned me in advance that I must call him 'Sir', something of a novelty for me as I'd had no pastors and masters hitherto. The interview chiefly consisted in a verbal spelling test which I passed with comparative ease until he came to one of his most difficult words: 'privilege' which, after some hesitation, I ended with '-A-G-E'. I was so preoccupied with trying to get it right that I quite forgot to call him 'Sir' but was nevertheless accepted and therefore due to leave Miss Jones's at the end of the Easter term. As I should thereafter be studying Latin Miss Jones got Father to find out the name of the Latin Primer I'd be using and started me on that. Thanks to her I was already 'into' languages at the age of nine, and for that matter into History, Painting, Poetry, and Music as well. There can't have been many schools in the Romford district where I could have done so much in the time.

Every day started with a hymn and a prayer. Each morning, on arrival, we gathered in the schoolroom upstairs while she gave a piano lesson – usually to Margaret Channon – in the drawing-room downstairs. When the lesson was over she rang a little handbell, the signal for us to troop down, pick up a words copy of *Hymns Ancient and Modern* as we entered and assemble in three short rows. She had no inhibitions about uttering prayers aloud, though I have little recollection of what she actually said; probably something to the effect 'Keep us this day without sin'. What did impinge were the hymns; they were 'Church of England' hymns and I thought some of them simply lovely. To bring back with the fullest force those days in the spring of 1917 it needs only the sound of a choir singing 'O happy band of pilgrims' for me to see the cretonne-covered armchairs in that little drawing-room, the pictures of Vermeer's 'Girl with a pearl ear-ring' and Velasquez's 'Infante Baltasari Carlos' on the wall and recall the wallflowers, the Solomon's Seal, the London Pride, and the Lily of the Valley in her tiny front garden. They form one powerful, composite memory and much of my childhood seems enshrined in it. With death and my day of reckoning approaching I feel an impulse to utter . . . not a prayer for her soul, which can hardly be in danger – God must in any case be assumed to know His own business – but thanks, gratitude, appreciation, and if there is anything in those immeasurable dimensions that encompass us which can be identified with what was once 'Miss Jones' I should like 'her' – and 'God' – to know of it.

The War

'Man is born free', said Rousseau, 'and everywhere he is in chains. In the ambience of the French *ancien régime* it will have sounded most convincing; certainly what 'everyone' wanted to hear. Now, when many of the chains he had in mind have been shed, partly thanks to him, we can see more clearly that Man is everywhere born in a whole entanglement of chains – iron, silken, golden – of race, tradition, class, parentage, temperament, public opinion . . . a creature born free of these would be sub-animal; most animals learn from their parents and are influenced by aspects of 'tribe'. Very few humans escape being born into some sort of tradition; heirs and sometimes victims. Remembering the poetry I learnt as a child, both at Miss Jones's and at the City of London School, I can see it as a golden chain that binds the generations, a canon of received treasure of the sort which does much to form a civilisation, or at least give it its savour. In this respect I regard myself as an heir. In many ways I was lucky.

In other respects, however, I was less so. One chain which none of us can escape is the zeitgeist we were born into. It is formative throughout our lives and when I consider my own fate in this respect I count myself and my contemporaries as victims. That odious nationalist/Imperialist hubris that disfigured the turn of the century was a disease of European civilisation and the war in which it unsurprisingly culminated in some ways marked the end of that civilisation. It seemed to us more odious in goose-stepping Berlin than elsewhere but in fact it was France's revanchist diplomacy after the war of 1870 that made the Great War almost inevitable. Moreover Kaiser Wilhelm's decision to increase the size of Germany's fleet was influenced by the fact of the Boer War, that attempt to extend 'wider still, and wider' our already enormous empire which aroused condemnation throughout Europe. When war was declared in 1914 there was cheering in Paris and London as well as Berlin. War was still regarded by most people as, at the least, a necessary evil, and by nearly everyone as manly and courageous especially among those Powers that regarded themselves as Great. As for pacifisim, it was not merely effeminate, it bordered on treason. Young men in all countries aspired to be Heroic, to transcend the dull routine of daily life, and few had taken into account the ever-increasing destructiveness of modern war. A war poem which later got itself remembered was 'The Volunteer' by Herbert Asquith:

> Here lies the clerk who half his life had spent
> Toiling at ledgers in a city grey,
> Thinking that so his life would drift away
> With no lance broken in life's tournament;
> Yet ever 'twixt the books and his bright eyes
> The gleaming eagles of the legions came,
> And horsemen, charging under phantom skies,
> Went thundering past beneath the oriflamme.

Too many people thought of war in such romantic terms, and many more found peace-time boring. A war would make an exciting change, a war which naturally 'we' would win (the poem ends with 'Who goes to join the men of Agincourt' and Agincourt – for the English – was a Famous Victory). Very few faced up to the possibility of defeat; still less did they consider that by regarding the Nation as 'sacred' they were not only breaking the 1st Commandment but making a sensible peace settlement impossible. A little common sense around the time of fraternisation at Christmas, 1914, could have restored Europe to health but people who were convinced that God looked with particular favour on their own Nation found this too heretical to contemplate and butchered their best men by the thousand rather than change their religion.

Wisdom after the event, of course, though in fact many thoughtful people throughout Europe had foreseen the tragedy. As a child of my time I imbibed some of the heady brew listening to May Chipperfield reciting 'England, my England', and imbibed more when the sound of a band proclaimed that another 'draft' of soldiers were marching to the station en route for 'the front', a signal for Nellie, and all the other maids in the neighbourhood – and a good many other people besides – to rush out into South Street, line the pavements and cheer, or call out facetious farewells, but from a higher source I learnt that many Liberals had voiced their objection to that earlier Boer War. On one of our walks Father had pointed out a house where the then minister of the Congregational church had lived and told me that he'd been dubbed what was termed 'pro-Boer', i.e. had deplored the folly of the Jameson Raid and the unnecessary war which followed it, and had his windows stoned by an angry mob in consequence. That such mobs should be active was another odious aspect of that time: the gutter press. A rose we had in the garden was officially named 'Daily Mail' since that newspaper had awarded it a prize for the best new rose of the season but such was the contempt that Father and the Aunts felt for 'that awful rag' that they avoided calling the rose by that name, even though it smelt as sweet. The activities of such Press Lords as Northcliffe, Beaverbrook, Rothermere . . . – the list is not yet closed – make disgusting showing and they were not then offset by the BBC.

By the time I was rising six I had no doubt that the French, being our Gallant Allies, were Good and that the Germans were Bad, indeed for most people Very Bad Indeed. Not that my parents were the sort to fulminate against the Germans, though I once heard Mother declare herself 'very angry with the Kaiser' (as no doubt Queen Victoria would have been) but since we talked frequently to Nellie, as well as hearing people talk in shops and elsewhere, we inevitably picked up what the gutter press was saying. The press Lords were in any case fond of printing letters charged with hate from 'respectable' people who should have know better, such as Rudyard Kipling. More direct evidence of German wickedness came with the Zeppelin raids but when I probe my very earliest memories I find myself recalling that we had a German living next door.

His name was Mr Espenschied, a burly 'Bavarian' with dark, curly hair, married to an Englishwoman of little distinction. I picked up somehow – probably from an overheard conversation with Aunt Elsie – that Mother regarded her as 'common'. Their youngest daughter, Joey (presumably short for Johanna), was a childhood playmate and in the unquestioning way of children I accepted this unusual name for a girl. Mother spoke of Mr Espenschied as 'rather a nice man' but I only recall seeing him once, across the fence between our two gardens when he was attending to one of his beehives. He clapped his hands to attract my attention as I was running down the garden, and said something to me but I couldn't understand the funny way he spoke English and said nothing back. As I was only three years old this was hardly surprising and I had no opportunity for further communication as very soon he was no longer to be seen in the garden or anywhere else. I learnt that he'd been 'interned' and gathered that this was something like 'put in prison'. Later the rest of his family left too and I no longer had Joey as a playmate but, right at the start of the war, I'd had it on parental authority that some Germans could be 'rather nice' and such authority overrode Aunt Alice's deep dislike, not to say hatred, of the Prussian militarism of Kaiser Wilhelm's Germany.

Childish memory is so patchy that it is hard to be sure of the sequence of events, and so of the year in which they happened. Hearsay about a distant phenomenon like 'the war' impinges far less than exciting events like summer holidays. My knowledge of the Great Eastern was not entirely confined to its suburban trains. 'Holidays' could mean catching an 'express' with a deep blue engine and steaming off through unfamiliar countryside past places with funny names such as Tiptree and Diss, changing at a junction called North Walsham to a branch line, and we were in fact in Mundesley when that war was declared. I can hardly say I remember it being declared but I do have a mental snapshot of a group of men in straw boaters, one of them with an open newspaper, discussing something very earnestly. Mother later said that several people had broken off their holidays and returned home but that Father had thought it more sensible to finish the holiday off. I agreed with him.

Father was by then well over forty and so not in danger of being 'called up' though the calling up of others meant that he had to put in a lot of overtime at the office. Later in the war – it must have been in 1917/18 – we went for two years running to Overstrand, Norfolk, and by that time food shortage was acute and we had to take our ration books. When, for one of our meals, our landlady, Mrs Clare, gave us fried plaice, it was regarded as an exceptional luxury. Another time she tapped at the window and said, 'I've got yer some bloa'ers!' (Do bloaters still exist? Those serried ranks of smoked herrings spiked through the gills with a stick were a familiar feature of every fishmonger's but I haven't seen any for years.) One day we walked the two miles to Cromer where Mother scoured the town in search of things to eat and came back with a packet called 'Turban Puddings' containing powder which one heated up with water to make a 'milk pudding' but it turned out to be a thin and not very sweet gruel rather like tapioca pudding and was not regarded as a success.

Details like these are more sharply engraved than the sight of warships in the North Sea. We noticed them, certainly, and the strange green, grey and mustard patterns painted on them. I even picked up the word 'camouflage' though I found it hard to understand how this could disguise them; it seemed to me to make them more conspicuous, but although I can still see them in my mind's eye and knew them to be connected with 'the war', hence a little sinister, they made less impression than 'Lady Battersea's Gardens', another vignette of that vanishing Edwardian period which can still supply the stuff of dreams. Lady Battersea was the lady of the manor and her gardens were one day thrown open to the public as a means of fund-raising for Wounded Soldiers while she sat at the receipt of custom wearing a vast hat laden with flowers and fruit. Pen's attempts to memorise Kipling's 'Our England is a garden' had given me ideas about 'lawns and avenues' and 'statues on the terraces', and when I happened to stray into a little bower where there was a pool with a blue mosaic floor and a fountain playing, the whole surrounded by scarlet and purple fuchsias and the smell of box, I felt a sincere 'O, how beautiful!'.

Looking back one tends to count the sunny hours, no doubt because these are the best remembered, but I don't recall being very conscious of hardship. Turban Pudding wasn't much fun, certainly, but we didn't go hungry (though I now wonder whether our parents sometimes did so that we shouldn't). We did, however, exploit every opportunity of living off the land and one day spent some very unsunny hours blackberrying near East Runton. Some of the Aunts had joined us and it was supposed to be a picnic but although it shortly came on to rain, and did so for the rest of the day, they were not deterred. They came well supplied with mackintoshes and umbrellas and thanks to these, and the shelter of some close-packed fir trees, we had our picnic in spite of the rain, indeed the *urbs in rure* charm of picnics was enhanced by the presence of household gods amid the sweet smell of wet blackberries. Thereafter we blackberried unceasingly and returned with a large basketful, together with some maggoty windfall apples found neglected in the wet grass on the edge of an orchard and Mrs Clare duly stewed these for us. The sugar shortage meant that they were on the sour side but this was offset by custard and we ate them contentedly while the grown-ups talked about 'sugar beet', a strange unheard-of crop which 'we', apparently hadn't much cultivated though the Gernnans had.

'Overstrand' was dream material not only for me but for our cousins next door, Isabel and Sandy. As the holiday approached our excitment became almost uncontainable and on the night before we were due to start, when packing had been completed, we had the greatest difficulty in going to sleep. The need to return to Romford at the end of it was a moment of torment, only compensated for by the exciting prospect of another 'long' railway journey. Even this long-distance train, however, didn't have corridor coaches and

Mother urged me to 'go' at North Walsham station as I shouldn't have another chance before we reached Romford.

She will have had in mind another earlier holiday in Swanage (which calculation shows to have been in 1915) when I was a mere four so that travelling on the London & South-Western Railway will have made less impression. What made it unforgettable was the fact that towards the end of it I badly wanted to 'go', so much so that when the train for some reason came to a standstill outside a station Father opened the carriage door a little and told me to go out of that. It was a sensible solution but I was horribly inhibited by the presence of another family in our compartment and still more by the fact that there were houses close by with a woman watching to see what was happening. I therefore failed to go before the train started again but by that time I could contain myself no longer so Father seized some sheets of newspaper, rolled them into a horn and told me to pee in that. I did so while the family at the other end of the compartment politely looked out of their window and pretended not to notice. When the horn was brimful Father threw it out of the window and I can still see it emptying itself as it fell towards the line.

It must have been in 1916 that I made my sole excursion on the London & North-Western before it became part of the London, Midland & Scottish, being taken by Grannie and Aunt Catherine to stay with 'Aunty Jessie' in the Lake District. The prospect of a long railway journey by night was certainly exciting but less so because Pen and my cousins were not coming too, and because Grannie and Aunt Catherine – her youngest but one daughter – were both rather strict. A further dampener was the increasing misery of the war, of which I was becoming aware. Our compartment was dismally lit and although, for once, it had a corridor, there was no question of a sleeping-car. Even in peace-time these were for 1st Class passengers and during the war they were all made available for hospital trains. The compartment was full but two of the passengers were wounded soldiers, one with his arm in a sling, the other with a leg encased in plaster, and the atmosphere was glum and far from holiday-like. The silence –

apart from the rhythmical clump of the wheels – plus the fact that there was only night to be seen out of the windows, made me bored though at one point the black sky was lit glaring read; 'blast furnaces making munitions', Aunt Catherine said.

In the end I did go to sleep and came to the surface again in the early morning and in Penrith station. There we changed to a train on the Cockermouth, Keswick & Penrith Railway and from that point onwards I felt myself in fairyland, seeing quite a different 'mountainous' country, stopping at Troutbeck and being reminded, by Aunt Catherine's singing, that this was where John Peel lived 'once on a day', and on the last lap running alongside Bassenthwaite Lake itself. Aunty Jessie was waiting on the platform with her sister Jeannie but we couldn't immediately proceed as the way was blocked by level-crossing gates and the train was about to start again. When it finally chuffed out a man in the signal box lustily turned a large wheel and the gates swung open untouched by human hand! In a ditch beside the footpath real live watercress was growing – hitherto known only from shops – and we picked some and had it for tea, a real North Country tea with scones and apple tart made by Aunty Jessie. There were no food shortages here. A farm close by supplied butter, milk, eggs, and now and again a rabbit or even a chicken. There were also no Zeppelin raids. From the windows of their little cottage we had a view of Skiddaw with its three knobs – when they were not hidden by clouds – and it was only a short walk to the lake where we were sometimes taken out in a boat by local boys who caught fish there. I gathered they were called 'bass' and assumed them to be the Bass in Bassenthwaite; and these we too took home for tea. One afternoon we had tea in the garden of the Pheasant Hotel, an old inn by the lakeside which had probably known the presence of John Peel in the past. Part of the tea was 'currant bread' but, innocuous though that was, I was conscious of entering what was in effect 'a pub' for the first time; my first experience of that age-old quietness with its ale-old smell.

One day I was invited to tea at – I think it was called Higham House – a very grand house with a pipe-organ in the hall! The sons of the house, of whom the older was five like me, had a nanny, as well as a vast garden, almost a park, with cedar trees. We had tea, with cucumber sandwiches, on one of the lawns and while we were having it saw a red squirrel scampering about in the branches of a nearby beech-tree. This by itself was unusual enough but our attention was arrested by a sudden plop on the lawn and we rushed up to look. It had actually missed its footing! It picked itself up at once and made for the tree but instead of running up the trunk it ran round and round until it came to its senses and headed upward!

After tea the older boy and I went for a walk in the woods which formed the further reaches of the vast garden. At a certain point he stopped, undid his flies and did an unashamed pee, grinning at me while he did it. This was clearly intended to introduce the interesting subject of what I later learnt were called 'pricks' but although in the past I'd sometimes been the one who introduced it, for some reason I hesitated to respond, perhaps because I felt he was even naughtier than I was, though I later reproached myself for being so cowardly. Later in the walk he revealed himself as positively wicked. We'd reached a steep hillside, dotted with occasional nesting-boxes where the local farmer allowed his chickens to range but the hens, in their casual way, would often lay their eggs in the tussocky ruts which terraced the hillside, so that collecting eggs meant a careful inspection of likely ruts. He was well aware of this and we found two or three eggs but instead of putting them into the nesting-boxes he said: 'Let's see how far we can throw them', and proceeded to hurl them as far as he could downhill so that they smashed on the hillside far below us. I finally returned home with a filthy white sailor-suit and a very guilty conscience even though I'd technically done nothing wrong myself. I knew it to be the more scandalous in wartime when eggs were daily becoming dearer and harder to get but I also suspected that I was potentially just as naughty, merely less daring.

There was one guilty secret, however, which I couldn't hide as it occurred at night and involuntarily; at the age of five I still hadn't stopped wetting the bed. Within the family it was an open secret and we'd come supplied with a piece of mackintosh to stretch below me in bed but I woke up one morning and heard Aunt Catherine say to Aunty Jessie 'He's wet the bed' and felt deeply humiliated, chiefly at the presence of Jessie who was new to the secret and whose bed it was. It was probably the humiliation which started my cure. Not long afterwards, back in Romford, I woke one morning without immediately opening my eyes and realised that I was on the very verge of wetting, followed by the further realisation that it must always be just before waking that I did it. It seemed to be a moment of 'truth', and the surfacing of it to consciousness somehow enabled me to connect up some alarm bell in my mind which operated thereafter as I ceased to wet my bed from that point onwards and it shortly became 'unthinkable'. This was sufficiently a landmark for me to associate it with my sixth birthday.

And in spite of the guilt and humiliation it was an unforgettable holiday which furnished my imagination for years. And to some extent still does; another powerful memory embalmed in its years. With Grannie, and Aunt Catherine and Aunty Jessie long since dead, and the shades of John Peel and an age-old England behind them, it seems to belong to another existence. Even in those quiet days I was conscious of the deep silence of the night; no trains, no cars, few horses and carts, only the pure country silence. Romford seemed a noisy, smokey place when I got back there and the war very much closer. Zeppelin raids were upon us. A fearful blurting siren fixed to the chimney of the police station warned of their approach, the signal to go downstairs and get under our mahogany dining-table while listening for the sinister droning of aircraft engines. Father and Uncle John, however, were too curious about it to remain indoors and ignoring the reproaches of their wives were constantly going outside to see whether anything had been caught in the ever-changing basket-work of searchlight beams.

One night it had; a brightly lit droning 'German sausage' which passed directly over us but fortunately didn't drop anything. On another night I found myself being rudely awoken by Father and resisted being thus disturbed but he nevertheless got me out of bed and took me to the back bedroom window where my sleepiness was at once forgotten. There was another, rather redder German Sausage in the sky beyond the housetops of Eastern Road and it shortly burst into flame, whereupon there was an outburst of cheering from the direction of the railway station and I suddenly realised that the night had been full of silent watchers and that there'd been a train in the station which had waited while all its passengers – and no doubt driver, stoker, guard and station staff – stood on the platform and watched.

First a few red-hot bits fell from it, then it slowly tilted and finally plunged flaming out of sight behind the roof-tops. Once the cheering had died down the train recalled itself to order and chugged off to Gidea Park, very late but with a good excuse. It was 'the one that came down at Billericay', hence about twelve miles away. It must have been a Friday night as the next day we went for a walk in the afternoon and when we reached the Brentwood Road (A.118) near Raphael Park we found it streaming with traffic. Everyone who had a vehicle was using it to head for Billericay, most of them on bicycles but many on motorbikes – Indians, Douglases, BSAs – and an astonishing number of cars – Fords, Singers, Daimlers, de Dion Boutons – we could hardly believe that so many cars existed. What the scrimmage was like at the scene of the crash was later reported in the Romford Recorder – Father read it out at the breakfast table – and for some weeks thereafter women were to be seen in the town wearing rings of zinc crudely fashioned out of purloined bits of wreckage. I also learnt that Germans had jumped from the airship rather than be burnt alive but the full horror was lost on me; it was exciting – and of course a Great Victory. Mother said that Father had missed the most exciting – when it was first hit – by going to wake me up. He'd evidently wanted me to witness such an usual spectacle.

One Sunday in Croydon we extended our walk home from church to look at 'bomb damage' caused by a recent air-raid to some houses in Cherry Orchard Road, and the sight of a bedroom wall blown out, with a brass bedstead sagging out of the gaping hole was an unprecedented and horrifying one. A home would no longer be a castle! The evidence stared us in the face, and I realised that part of the magic of the Lake District had been that it was 'too far for the Germans to come'.

The first time Father took us to see 'Peter Pan' I overheard Mother reporting to Aunt Elsie that Mrs Patrick Campbell had played the part of Mrs Darling but he took us again the following year and it was one of the most outstanding events of my childhood though I was disappointed to find that Peter was being played by a girl, a 'principal boy' with the funny name of Faith Celli (no doubt the boys were all at the front). I was nevertheless entirely swept away and flying figured in my dreams, and in my waking imagination, for years. When it came to 'Clap your hands all who believe in fairies' I clapped with the utmost ardour though in less carried-away moments I was already beginning to doubt their existence.

Within the theatre 'the war' was utterly forgotten but these visits to 'town' were exceptional in giving me a whiff of 'London by Night', quite a different experience from Mother's daytime shopping expeditions to D.H Evans and Marshall & Snelgrove. After the show we were taken, as a special Christmas treat, to a very grand tea-shop called Buszard's to have as sumptuous a tea as wartime allowed and on the way there passed women, some of them with painted faces, on the arms of soldiers and dressed – I knew it from the Aunts' fitting-room pictures – far more fashionably than was usual at Romford and drifting the scent of 'Lily of the Valley' or 'Parma Violets'. I at once sensed what I'd heard grown-ups talk about as 'immorality' and it was further enhanced by the smells from the ill-ventilated Tube. At the entrance to any of its stations, and still more when one went down in a lift, a smell puffed up which I felt to be in some way 'wicked' and no less so for being sometimes mingled with the soldier's cigar-smoke.

With Father too old to be conscripted and his brother John merely called to a clerical job when the over-40s were called up, the only remaining male in the family was Uncle John Bryson, admittedly in the Royal Flying Corps but as he had remarkably bad sight there was little danger of his being used as an aviator. As a result we 'lost' nobody but I could hardly fail to be aware of others less lucky, particularly at church: Mrs Craig in deep mourning, and later Mrs Clark and Mrs Harris likewise in black and in tears at the services. These were made further miserable by the inclusion in every service of 'Litanies' whose words were pasted in the front and back of every hymnbook: 'Eternal Father, strong to save' in supplication 'for those in peril on the sea', and 'God, the all-terrible' (to the tune of the Czarist national anthem) which ended 'Give to us peace in our time, O Lord', but despite this weekly beseeching throughout the land the Lord appeared to take very little notice.

Nevertheless while the war lasted people resorted to the Church to a greater extent than in peace-time and it became common to see people, particularly women in mourning, who'd never been seen previously. One Sunday there was one in *our pew*! There was in fact plenty of room for her but knowing that it was our pew made me feel indignant and I made a whispered expostulation to Mother, despite the fact that the woman smiled at me. Mother whispered back 'Poor woman! She's probably lost somebody in the war'. This was a new thought, enough to swing my feelings to the opposite extreme, and I felt a great surge of pity for her. Poor, *poor* woman, I thought, nearly in tears about it, and thereafter wanted to be kind to her. This spectacular 'conversion' was in its way quite a landmark in my spiritual life; it had a permanent influence on my attitude to strangers. Mother had got the message across at the right moment.

The misery of the war increased as it went eternally on, and four years could only be felt as an eternity. The ever-mounting death-roll could be seen in the black dresses for women and black arm-bands for men, quite apart from food shortages and increasing prices in shops, and behind them was a feeling of hopelessness which could infect us even without our being aware of the source. It registered more directly whenever we went anywhere by train. One of the small pleasures of a railway station in normal times was its automatic machines. For a penny one could get a bar of chocolate, or weigh oneself, or stamp one's name on a piece of aluminium tape and take it home, but in the course of the war these articles dried up and the machines were always empty, the drawers fixed in the 'out' position, thus covering up the slot and making it impossible to put a penny in. As the war dragged on I used to wonder whether they would *ever* have anything in them again, and could see no prospect of it.

Then, one Sunday evening late in 1917, an event occurred which, though independent of the war, heavily increased the misery. Sitting at supper in Aunt Elsie's back room – she'd let the front rooms as a source of income in Uncle's absence – we heard the front door bell ring and a telegram arrived which she read out: MOTHER VERY ILL BRYSON. To me it was a first incomprehensible; 'Bryson' normally meant me and Mother was clearly not very ill but the reactions of Mother and Aunt Elsie soon made its meaning apparent. After some hurried consultation between them Mother appeared in her outdoor clothes. Her last act before hurrying to the station was to fill a hot-waterbottle and looking up I saw a tear trickling down her cheek. Incredulously I asked, 'Are you crying, Mother?', being under the impression that grown-ups never cried. She said, 'Well, wouldn't you cry if your mother was dying?' and at this I hugged her to me, unable to bear the thought.

Grannie's illness was a stroke and after an agonised week or two, during which letters were exchanged and read out at our end, a further stroke carried her off. When the time came for the funeral Mother took me to Croydon with her; normally an exciting event and I felt proud of myself for being singled out for the privilege though in fact the reason was little to my credit. Mother and Elsie couldn't both attend as one of them would have to look after 'the children' and since Isabel, with her short straight hair like a boy's, was only four and Sandy barely two, Elsie was the obvious candidate for doing so but such was my reputation for naughtiness and 'setting Isabel a bad example' that she didn't want the responsibility of coping with me as well.

As a result I was the only young person present. Nevertheless, by then seven years old, I took it all in and it supplied further abiding memories. No. 60 Dingwall Road was quiet at the best of times and in the presence of death, with all the blinds drawn, it was as hushed as the tomb itself. In such an atmosphere naughtiness was out of the question. At a certain point Mother took me by the hand into the best bedroom where the coffin lay and for the first time I looked on death. It was not a pretty sight. The skull showed through the grey skin and irregular teeth were visible. If Mother had reacted with shocked horror I should have done the same but as she simply surveyed the body with reverent sorrow; I took my cue and did likewise – and never forgot the sight. I noticed her full name inscribed on the coffin lid: 'Alice Stewart Bryson, née Glegg, aged 68 years', the more noteworthy as we were never allowed to know the ages of grown-ups and here, in the presence of death, the secret was fully revealed.

Next morning horse-drawn carriages clopped up to the pillared front door, waited until the undertaker's men bore the coffin to the hearse and mourners each in turn stepped on the ornamental foot-rests which curved below each carriage door, and we then clopped all the way to Mitcham cemetry, I privately delighted at this exciting ride in a smart carriage. In due course we stood around the grave in the rain, Mother still holding my hand; at the words 'Ashes to ashes, dust to dust' the undertaker's man poured handfuls of earth onto the lowered coffin and Uncle John Bryson sobbed audibly while more of my childish notions were undermined. If it had been startling that Mother should cry it was even more so that a man should. It was a jeer against any child to be called a 'crybaby', particularly a boy, and for a *man*! . . . We climbed back into the carriages and clopped rather faster back to Dingwall Road. After a lunch at which the oval dining table was more crowded than usual we repaired to the be-mirrored drawing-room where he read out the will while his sisters listened reverently (an occasion of which I was obliged to remind him many years later).

Thereafter death became something much thought about. The seamstresses told me that Grannie would have gone 'straight to heaven' but since my family grown-ups were less hot for such certainties this answer came as somewhat dusty. At church we sometimes sang the hymn 'Rock of Ages' which I found very affecting, and the line 'When my eye-strings break in death' provided a startling image. Another much more maudlin hymn which was sometimes unearthed – probably for the benefit of the bereaved – was:

> A widowed mother lost her son.
> She had no son beside.
> He was her loved, her only one,
> And he fell sick and died.

It was one of a mid-nineteenth-century vintage engendered by the popularity of Dickens's 'Death of Little Nell' but for me it was no laughing matter; in the prevailing grief both at church and at home I found it easy to weep too. I then discovered a song in the music cabinet:

> O Father, dear Father, come home to me now.
> The clock in the steeple strikes one.
> You promised, dear Father, that you would come home
> As soon as your day's work was done.

It was a Band of Hope song (with a waltz rhythm) intended to shame fathers who squandered their substance at the pub while their indigent families starved in squalor at home but it reduced me to tears at the thought 'Wouldn't it be terrible if Father *never* came home!'. My parents found me crying, and, on discovering the reason, put the song out of harm's way. I detected a little quiet amusement that I should be so affected by a cheap song but by that time I was deep in the misery groove.

Then, for good measure, there was another death in the family. Aunt Catherine, who'd been nursing war-wounded at Plaistow Hospital, caught menegitis and was 'very ill' for a long time. Few people then had telephones but Mr Vincent, who'd succeeded to my grandfather's veterinary business next door, was an exception and it became a daily event, on those dark mornings when the war was at its worst, for Ellen, the Vincents' maid, to come hurrying to our back door, the signal for either Mother or Aunt Elsie to go and take the call while we children went on eating our porridge. By the time it came to Aunt Elsie reporting one morning, in a broken voice, 'She's gone' it was no surprise to anyone. We sat and ate in silence. There must have been a funeral but I didn't attend it. It will have been Aunt Elsie's turn.

'Russia'

'Russia' crept into my ken via Tchaikowsky's 'Album for the Young'. Even before I was set to work on 'The New Doll' I used to wake up in the morning and hear Pen practising 'The Song of the Lark'. Tchaikowsky's name was printed in large Gothic letters across the front of the album and wasn't easy to pronounce, or even to read, but Pen reported Miss Barber as saying 'It's a cross between a cough and a sneeze – or rather a sneeze and a cough'. The music, however, presented no such difficulties; 'The Song of the Lark' sounded brilliant when Pen played it though I later discovered that it wasn't really very hard, and the same applied to 'Neapolitan Song'.

Around the same time the Sunday School organised their annual entertainment and I was conscripted to act in a playlet called 'Where Love is God is'. This was by 'Tolstoy', a much easier name. I had to play the part of a cobbler who looked out of his basement window and commented on the footwear he saw walking past, the owners of which he could identify thanks to his trade. The play was evidently a success as there was a repeat open-air performance in 'Mr Mann's fields', just off Petit's Lane. Judging by the compliments afterwards the play was a deeply moving occasion but I hadn't yet learnt that congratulations on such occasions were not always to be taken at their face value.

Then, with 'The Revolution', Russia swam into everybody's ken and I picked up a good deal (much more than I realised at the time) through hearing Father read out the news at the breakfast table. Strange names and words occurred which he sometimes had to guess the pronunciation of, one of them 'Bolshevik' though this soon caught on and became acclimatised and shortened into the adjective 'bolshy'. One day it was given an unexpected slant by Pen. When she left Miss Jones's Pen was sent to the City of London School for Girls and (amazing though it now seems for a little girl of nine!) commuted daily to London by train. When she got home in the afternoon she had a way of prattling loquaciously about the girls and the mistresses, their names and the things they said and as usual I listened attentively. The school had a London peculiarity: it had a high percentage of Jews, and one girl whose remarks were often reported was named Florrie Bernstein. It shortly became clear that Florrie knew a lot about the goings-on in Russia – evidently reflecting her parents' preoccupations – and she pronounced the word 'Bolshevik' with the accent on the second syllable. One day Pen reported her as saying: 'They say the Bolshéviks do this and the Bolshéviks do that and it's all lies because they *don't* do it' (I find it surfacing thus verbatim from Pen's account). Apart from this there was no suggestion that Florrie spoke other than fluent and authentic English and at this distance it is easy to guess that she must have been one of a second generation of refugees from the pogroms of the turn of the century for whom the main enemy would still be Czarism but I doubt if I appreciated this at the time. Nevertheless I remember the incident very clearly though I find Pen has quite forgotten it.

By this time Father's readings from the newspapers included a good deal about 'refugees' and one day some real live ones turned up in Romford. I attended a weekly dancing class, held in the church hall, where we were instructed in such dances as the Highland Fling, the Sailor's Hornpipe, and Sir Roger de Coverley but there was also girls' ballet class which we could sit and watch. I was carried away by their stiff gauze skirts and their neat little legs twinkling below and one evening two newcomers appeared who were clearly outstanding. Their names, I learnt, were Lani and Sonya Ephgrave. I must have been told that they were Russian refugees but I was chiefly aware of their being so exotic. Not long afterwards, in South Street, looking into the window of a sweet-shop with Isabel, I saw one of them inside it and, proud of my knowledge, said to

Isabel, 'You see that girl there. Her name's Lani Ephgrave' and then noticed that a man standing behind me was looking at me most curiously. It struck me that he must be her father but nothing more happened. Perhaps I added 'She's in our dancing class' so that he had no need to enquire how I knew. I wondered whereabouts they were living in Romford and wished I could get to know them.

Once 'the war' was over events in Russia were even more in the news and one day the Daily News had a whole-page spread of a map of the 'Civil War' front which Father cut out, stuck on a piece of cardboard and hung on the dining-room wall, clearly regarding it as Important, as well as immediately available for the identification of place-names. Before it was hung up Pen lent it further importance by painting the White Sea Chinese White and the Black Sea Lamp Black. If the Red Sea had appeared on it she would certainly have painted that Vermilion or Crimson Lake; Contingents of British soldiers had been sent there via 'Archangel' – a much easier name. Names of individuals were also read out, many of them not easily pronounced though 'Lenin' was an exception; 'Trotsky' too, being such a funny name. All this formed the background to names like Florrie Bernstein, and Lani and Sonya Ephgrave.

Then, one Sunday, most exceptionally, an announcement was made at church of a film to be shown at the Victory Palace, our local 'fleapit'. Mother and Father didn't greatly approve of the cinema – though it already excited me – but this was a 'charity' performance organised by the Save the Children Fund and we were encouraged to attend it. It was about refugees, but not bourgeois immigrants; it concerned the terrible sufferings of the Russian people and we were shown pictures of starving children and destitute mothers and soup kitchens; a silent film, of course, but a woman addressed us with a spoken commentary in the course of which we heard another, no doubt more correct, pronunciation of some of the place-names. There was also a shot of a whole train, complete with its locomotive, embedded in deep snow though I was more struck by the fact that one of the underfed children was stark naked; an unprecedented sight in a film.

It was followed up by a flag-day, likewise organised at the church, and Pen, aged about twelve, was conscripted to sell flags. This required her to be up early enough to catch the early morning trade at the railway station and as I was greatly interested I accompanied her. It was as well I did so. Unbeknown to any of us she was sickening for scarlet fever and at an early point, standing by the entrance to the Up-platform, she said to me 'I think I'm going to faint' and did. I tried to hold her up but was dismayed to find how heavy an unconscious twelve-year-old could be and only succeeded in preventing her from falling; she sagged to the ground. Various kindly persons at once offered help and the man who ran the coffee-stall alongside held an enamel mug of water to her mouth though she didn't drink it – later reporting that the mug looked so dirty. And when she'd recovered I took her home where Mother, much perturbed, at once put her to bed.

Meanwhile here was her tray of flags still unsold so I took it over and spent the rest of the day selling flags for Russians. In the course of it I got talking to a girl from church who'd been similarly conscripted and who said 'I *must* remember to say "Will you help the starving children" because if you say " . . . the starving *Russian* children" lots of people won't help'. News of the doings of Lenin, Trotsky, Denikin, Kolchak and the rest had evidently given 'Russia' such a bad name that the uttering of it was an excuse for not wanting to know. Russia had clearly become a major topic of conversation and as I was rising ten it was less surprising that it should make an impression but I chiefly acquired a sense of 'disaster' from grown-ups. Full sense would be made of it later but its measure had been taken.

The same applied, even more strongly, to the Great War. Much reading and many photographs have since filled in details of which I was unaware at the time but 'filled in' is the operative expression; the emotional background was there and has remained there. It was reinforced in 1922 when D.W. Griffiths' film 'The Four Horsemen of the Apocalypse' of the book by Vicente Blasco Ibanez, with Rudolf Valentino, Lewis Stone,

Adolphe Menjou, and Alice Terry, affected me so powerfully that I saw it five times, the first time in the company of Mother who, most exceptionally, took us to London to see it at the Palace Theatre in Cambridge Circus. There it could be given the full treatment with red flashes on the screen at the moment of an explosion and colossal off-stage bangs to synchronise with them, a treatment unobtainable at the Victory Palace.

Music had a good deal to do with this profound impression as the film, although 'silent', was exceptional in taking its music programme with it. Even the Victory Palace, when in due course it arrived there, had to expand its tiny 'orchestra' for the occasion. As a result I had several hearings of a brief passage for strings which struck me so forcibly and came back to me so clearly that I managed – thanks to Miss Barber – to write it down, and in the right key. Mother showed this to Madame Snell who identified it as the beginning of Beethoven's 'Coriolanus' Overture and she obtained a piano solo version of it for me to play.

It was really far too difficult for me, and in any case not at all pianistic, but I slaved at it much more assiduously than at most of my pieces and for a long time couldn't dissociate it from screen captions in art nouveau lettering: 'And so, through the muck and mire of a man-created hell, went Madariaga's grandsons; the one a Frenchman . . .' (cut to a moonlight blue, heavily-raining scene in no-man's-land with Rudolf Valentino in a French soldier's helmet crawling through the mud and barbed wire) 'the other, a German . . .' (Cut to a very smiliar scene with somebody else in a German helmet) ' . . . till a stray shell puffed out their lives', followed by a screened explosion, red flash and deafening detonation, followed shortly by Alice Terry reading aloud to Lewis Stone who, I fancy, had been blinded in the war, with a sad tune called 'Forever and forever' being played in the background. You could tell she was reading aloud because you could see her lips moving.

Silent films by now mostly seem so ludicrous that it is only the comedies which will bear resuscitation and it is hard to believe that we once found them so moving but I was far from being the only one; the film was 'a sensation' and must have netted millions. It seems very possible that 'Journey's End', the play by R.C. Sherriff, would now seem less moving than it did c.1930 but there's no doubt that then it moved me to the core of my being – as it did a million others. In tune with the zeitgeist I devoured all the books about the war published around that time, Remarque's 'All quiet on the Western Front' making the greatest impression. Hitler and his war then pushed the First World War into the background and provided material for other films which in due course will no doubt seem – sometimes already do seem – naif or absurd.

After the Second World War the First remained in abeyance until the mid-1960s when Joan Littlewood, inspired by Charles Chilton, put on 'O, what a lovely war!' and I found myself moved all over again. And again it was chiefly music that did the trick; the reminder of 'Keep the home fires burning', 'Pack up your troubles in your old kit-bag', 'There's a long, long trail' and others, seemed to unearth my very roots. Such was its success that a film was made of it too, and I find myself wondering how far that film will stand the test of time. I saw it as recently as 1970 – in Rome of all places! – and it was not only the music which moved me but a sequence at the end where the ghosts of dead soldiers, in khaki, walk silently past, behind their still living relatives; a bereaved mother sitting in the grass feels rather than sees her dead son in the vicinity but he passes wordlessly behind her and at the very end is seen with a crowd of his trenchmates, all of whom then dissolve into crosses. A skilful bit of film technique, certainly. It moved me to such uncontrollable tears that when we went for a much-needed drink afterwards I caused general embarrassment and was quite unable to explain the depths of my emotion.

And all this depite the fact that, as a family, we'd been 'alright Jack'. Father having had to do a great deal of overtime in the course it, had saved up enough money to enable him, a few years later, to build a new and very much nicer house in the Surrey stockbroker belt. The move there, in 1923, didn't quite mark the end of childhood – one is hardly a young man at the age of thirteen – but it did mark the end of a chapter by distancing 'the war' into an increasingly remote Romford past and making it more easily forgotten. The past, however, is not so easily disposed of.

While the fate of 'Russia' does not strictly move me to tears, her 'disaster' remains a subject of abiding importance. Almost any book concerning that, for me, undiscovered country which covers the largest land mass on the globe, I read with intense interest and still deplore the fact that that conceited little terrorist Lenin, so cocksure that he was right and so lustful for power, should have deprived both her and us of each other's company for seven decades. The 'iron curtain' is an expression we associate with the aftermath of the Second World War but it was in fact drawn by Lenin – several hundred miles further east – at the Treaty of Brest-Litovsk in 1918.

Hymns, Prayers and Sermons

Lord Salisbury, writing in 1865, made an assertion which will have been endorsed by most of his readers: '. . . men will not be moral without a motive, and that motive can only be furnished by religious belief', though he allowed that 'for two or three generations . . . a standard of Christian conduct . . . might continue to be maintained by men who have renounced the faith'.

Since more than four generations have elapsed since he wrote that I feel a little uncertain which one I belong to though I do know that one of my earliest recollections is of 'family prayers' on Sunday mornings. At the appointed moment all of us, including Nellie, our maid, trooped into the drawing-room – Nellie for some reason always bearing her prayer book –, sat reverently while Father read some extract from the Bible, then got on our knees and buried our heads in chair or sofa cushions while he said a prayer. He was continuing a practice learnt from his own much-honoured but early-lost father, and even at that age I felt the 'reverence' to be slightly embarrassing but this won't have had anything to do with the fact that, for some reason, the practice ceased.

Not that religion became less important. An almost equally early memory is sitting, literally, at Mother's knee and hearing Bible stories. The Good Samaritan was my favourite; it was easy to see the moral of it. The Prodigal Son was certainly interesting but harder to see the point of; I knew I was sometimes naughty – though not *that* naughty – but I didn't understand why he was rewarded with the best robe and the fatted calf when he finally returned home. It was nevertheless a story and I never minded a story being repeated, indeed remember Pen objecting that I always wanted the Good Samaritan, and we heard these so often that they got lodged verbatim. Famous quotes such as 'He passed by on the other side' and 'He wasted his substance with riotous living' remained identifable and meaningful thereafter. As for church-going, I can hardly recall a time when it wasn't part of every Sunday morning's routine, and Bible stories at Mother's knee were soon succeeded by afternoon attendance at Sunday School. Church-going was still conventional – anyway for the middle classes; the working classes were not much represented at church – and those who didn't conform mostly kept quiet about the fact. The Gibsons never went near a church but if they sensed social disapproval for non-attendance they let it be known that they were Presbyterians, and Romford boasted no Presbyterian church. Our doctor, too, gave the impression that church-going was not for the likes of him but he had no partner to stand in for him and so could claim the exigencies of his profession.

To begin with I enjoyed it, and savoured the smell of Mother's lavender water, but for me it ended with the Children's Hymn, after which we children trooped out leaving the grown-ups to get down to some serious religion. When I was thought to be old enough to stay the full course – a process hastened by the nuisance of having to see me home and ensure that there was somebody to keep me out of mischief when I got there – I mostly found the sermon a deadly bore. Much more interesting were the hymns. We used the Congregational Church Hymnary and during the boredom of the sermon I was allowed to browse in the Bible or the hymnbook. Boards on each side of the church displayed the numbers of the hymns due for singing and one way of passing the time was to hunt up the next one due and find the place for the others in the pew. In the music version of the hymnbook every hymn showed the name of its author, with dates, and the composer of the tune, and as my musical appreciation advanced over the years I was one day surprised to notice that 'Onward, Christian soldiers' was by Sullivan and, at Christmas, that 'Hark, the herald angels sing' was by

Mendelssohn, both of them composers whose music I by that time knew from other sources.

To begin with the tune and its singability was everything but the words came as an inextricable part of the package and could often impinge, indeed were cemented into memory through being thus embedded. Church-going continued for many years, however, and it must have been during the earlier ones that two hymns singled themselves out by feeling 'different' from most:

> How pleased and blest was I
> To hear the people cry
>   'Come, let us seek our God to-day.
> Yes, with a cheerful zeal
> Hasten to Zion's hill
>   And there our vows and honours pay.

and there were several more verses to the same effect. The other was:

> Come, let us join our cheerful songs
>   With angels round the throne.
> Ten thousand, thousand are their tongues
>   But all their joys are one.

Both of these were by Isaac Watts[1] (1674–1748) but they stood out by their cheerfulness and it must have been in the earlier part of the war that we sang them. They would have seemed out of place in 1917/18. One arresting hymn in which words and music fitted like hand and glove was 'Fierce raged the tempest o'er the deep' and it was the first to make me conscious of bass parts. On the words 'raged the tempest' the organ bass thundered up the scale to imitate a surging billow, followed by a further and higher billow on 'o'er the deep' and I

1 Watts was a pioneer in the matter of hymns. In 1707 he published what was in effect the first English book of hymns – as opposed to metrical psalms – thereby setting a precedent later followed by all denominations.

was the more conscious of it as Mr Gardner, two pews behind, made a practice of singing the bass part, rather loudly. Another at first arrested because it started with exactly the same notes as 'Those evening bells' at Miss Jones's but its words nevertheless made a deep impression, perhaps through the association with the sight of a zeppelin caught in a blaze of searchlights:

> Eternal Light! Eternal Light!
> How pure the soul must be
> When, placed within the searching sight,
> It shrinks not but with calm delight
> Can live and look on thee!
>
> Thomas Binney, 1798–1874

I was reminded of it, years later, when singing in 'The Dream of Garontius' where Elgar exploits the maximum force of the orchestra – 'The Presence Chord' – for the moment of the soul's confrontation with God, followed by 'Take me away!' and the beautiful aria 'Softly and gently' to finish off the oratorio. One can discern a difference between those brought up to conceive of God as too Almighty and Majestic for a mere human being to confront and those whose inclusion among the Elect would entitle them to do just that, however awe-inspiring they might expect to find it, but the Congregationalists were not Predestinarians. Nor, for that matter, were they Fundamentalists who believed every word of the Bible to be literally true. One was expected to be reasonably knowledgable about one's beliefs.

Ever since I could remember I'd seen titles in Father's bookcase: 'Helps to the Study of the Bible', 'Dictionary of the Bible' by James Hastings, 'Ecce Homo' by J.R. Seeley, 'Whiston's Josephus' and others, and he sometimes talked of the Higher Criticism. It was through talking to him that I learnt about Predestinarians and Fundamentalists and automatically picked up his prejudices about them. I found he was rather contemptuous of Fundamentalism and when Pen later married into an Evangelistic family – though the son she married had hotly rebelled against it – I came to see why he was; they were guilty of Wilful Ignorance. They were very wealthy – as so often – yet incapable of a detached, well-informed discussion about religion; they didn't want to know. 'The Truth', i.e. the literal words of the Holy Writ – in English, naturally – was 'given' and nothing further was needed. Moreover they compounded their sin of Ignorance with that of Pride; they felt virtuous for thus refusing, looking down somewhat pityingly on those who didn't share their views and hadn't the slightest doubt about proselytising on all sides. Despite their wealth they didn't send their sons to the University because there they'd be in danger of losing their Faith, and Faith was everything. That they were uncultured and unlettered for people of their class and income was not a matter for which they felt any apology.

For Father this was sinning against the light; bowing down to the Bible as if it were so much wood and stone. Education was desirable in itself and the congregations he belonged to took care that their minister should be an educated man. He was '*Primus inter pares*' – First among Equals, Father explained – but he would be more spontaneously regarded as First if he could be respected for his learning. His sermons would also, with any luck, be more interesting to listen to.

Sermons were, of course, an essential part of every service and became more interesting as I got older, especially when they were informative as they sometimes were. The minister, when expounding the Scriptures, would often explain the background to a given text and supply historical detail, and although famous phrases from the King James Bible were known and loved the text was not regarded as sacrosanct. It was not uncommon for a minister to quote the Greek original of a word or phrase in pursuit of its real meaning. When considering a text, Father, who was Superintendent of the Sunday School, nearly always consulted Moffat's translation for an alternative reading.

Nevertheless of the hundreds of sermons I must have listened to I can only recall two and the first of these was only memorable for the fact that the minister declaimed his text:

'Come over to Macedonia and help us' (Acts, 16:9), at least half-a-dozen times in the course of it; his dramatic repetition of the words engraved them on my memory but what they illustrated got forgotten. The other, from a visiting minister, was more like an interesting history lesson than a sermon, its subject being those remarkable institutions: the Dissenting Academies, institutions of which I, and I suspect most of the congregation, had never heard though clearly an important strand in English social history.

It seems a little astonishing, in retrospect, that for centuries sermons were an important social institution; not only publicly preached but often later published. The 1910s were the last decade in history in which people had to bestir themselves in order to hear an unamplified human voice making pronouncements which were felt to be important, and would travel, often for miles, to hear an 'acoustic' speech by Mr Gladstone or Lloyd George. Since the 1920s we've been able to lie in bed and listen to it on the radio. By the 1910s, too, illiteracy had all but disappeared and political speeches could be read in the newspaper whereas in the past, sermons were among the few opportunities for the illiterate, or semi-literate, to hear the talk of an educated man.

Children's Hymns

Isaac Watts's name had arrested my attention as it wasn't new to me; another book in Father's bookcase was 'Divine Songs, attempted in Easy Language for the use of Children', a tiny book dated 1821, with charming engraved illustrations, which had formerly belonged to his grandmother.[1] I knew one or two of the 'songs' in it as they were also in our poetry book at Miss Jones's. One was 'How doth the little busy bee improve each shining hour' and another ''Tis the voice of the sluggard, I hear him complain "You have waked me too soon, I must slumber again"' but although I could imagine them as songs I didn't feel they really qualified as hymns, still less some of the other verses in other Songs:

> Oft we see a young beginner
> Practice little pilfering ways,

1 Watts was also a pioneer in publishing what was in effect the first children's hymbook – in 1715 – which 'averaged an edition every eighteen months for the next century and a half' (Scholes, P.A.: *Oxford Companion to Music*, Oxford University Press, 1945). It will no doubt have been attentive reading of the Bible that prompted the idea, notably the text in the tenth chapter of St Mark's gospel: 'Suffer little children to come unto me' and 'whosoever shall not receive the kingdom of God as a little child, he shall not enter therein'. It seems astonishing that it took so many centuries for Christians to act on this Authoritative injunction (perhaps the celibacy of the clergy had something to do with it) and the more so when one reads Watts's preface to the book which sets out the obvious reasons for getting 'a relish for virtue and religion in early' but children had no particular status in society and were given little attention in literature – apart perhaps from lullabies.

Till grown up a hardened sinner,
Then the gallows ends his days.

and it would have been interesting to learn what tunes the children of Watt's time sang to them to. Presumably, for eighteenth-century children, as for us, the tune would have been the most important part of the package but there was no knowing what they would have regarded as 'a lovely tune'. Our hymns and tunes were of a much later date and it would have been nice to know what he would have thought of some of them. One we enjoyed was:

Around the throne of God in heaven
   Thousands of children stand.
Their sins have long since been forgiven,
   A holy, happy band.
      Chorus: 'Singing Glory, Glory, Glory!' (twice)

It occured to me that to sit in a choir 'for ever and ever' singing nothing but 'Glory, Glory, Glory!' might pall after a couple of centuries but we sang it cheerfully enough for the length of the hymn. With its theme of adoring round the Throne one might have expected it to be by Watts but in fact it was written by Anne Shepherd (c.1857). Most of the Children's Hymns we sang were written by women in the mid-nineteenth century (and with a strong tendency to make the child the mouthpiece of their own reflections). I doubt whether I knew the word 'sentimental' but I seemed to catch a whiff of it and found some of these rather irksome:

We are but little children weak,
Nor born to any high estate.
What can we do for Jesus' sake
Who is so high and good and great?

As for 'There is a green hill far away', we thorougly disliked it though our objection was chiefly to the tune. The hymn was by a Mrs Alexander who was likewise responsible for 'Jesus calls us o'er the tumult' which we liked, as well as for 'All things bright and beautiful' which was even more popular.

One hymn which I found profoundly moving and seemed to epitomize 'church' was 'I think when I read that sweet story of old' by Jemima Luke. Her name first arrested my attention because Father tended to use 'Jemima' as a comic name for a woman but both words and music soon ousted this reaction and the last verse of it moved me deeply:

> But thousands and thousands who wander and fall
> Never heard of that heavenly home.
> I should like them to know there is room for them all,
> And that Jesus has bid them to come.

It appealed to my missionary instinct; the impulse to 'do good'. I liked to think of myself as being kind and helpful, without realising the assumption of superiority that this risked implying, quite apart from expecting gratitude, even admiration, for my efforts. As usual, however, it was just as much the tune that moved me. Its title was 'Athens' and instead of the name of the composer was written 'Greek Melody'. This was very unusual. I was beginning to learn about 'the Greeks' but this was not the sort of tune I'd have associated with what I'd learnt.[2] Not that our childish taste in music was any guide to their real worth. Some of the most popular tunes, especially at Sunday School, had a Moody and Sankey jauntiness:

> Jesus bids us shine with a pure clear light,
> Like a little candle burning in the night,

2 Research reveals that in fact the tune came first. Jemina Luke, a schoolmistress, came across it as a 'marching piece' for young children at the Normal Infant School in Grays Inn Road, London, and it so took her fancy that she set about devising words for it, beginning with the first two verses. The third verse, quoted above, was added later 'with missionary intent'! Well, she got her message across to me, nearly a century later, but I should still like to know more about the original 'Greek' tune.

He looks down from heaven to see us shine;
You in your small corner and I in mine.[3]

One Sunday just before the Second World War, out of politeness to a family I was staying with, I attended a Congregational Church service and for the Children's Hymn the minister announced 'Hymn No.730'. It turned out to be one of the ones I'd found sentimental:

God make my life a little light
Within the world to glow;
A little flame that burneth bright
Wherever I may go.

Matilda B. Edwards, 1873

but meanwhile the organist, using a mellow clarinet stop, was reminding us of the once-so-familiar tune and when it came to singing I found it impossible to join in; tears intruded uncontrollably and with them a reminder of 'Mother'. D.H. Lawrence wrote a poem about a very similar experience:

The glamour
Of childish days is upon me, my manhood is cast
Down in a flood of rememberance, and I weep
like a child for the past

3 This was written by Susan Warner (c.1867) whom research shows to have been an American. The zeitgeist clearly embraced both sides of the Atlantic.

Sunday School and the Boys' Brigade

Sunday School was quite different from church; it was a different class scene, one of its objects being to 'rescue' the children of working class parents who never went near a church, and some of them were pretty rough. Their parents had no great objection, being for the most part only too pleased to be quit of the children on a Sunday afternoon at the cost of a penny for the collection. One hymn in the Primary Section was:

See the pennies dropping,
  Dropping as they fall.
Every one for Jesus;
  He shall have them all.

sung while the collection was being taken and we gazed at framed reproductions of G.F. Watts's 'Light of the world' and of Jesus gathering 'the dear little children of every clime' to his arms. I used to wonder how the teachers managed to get the money into his hands but didn't doubt that the miracle was somehow achieved. Some of the children used to plead poverty and produce no penny but their breaths often smelt strongly of 'bull's eyes' or 'clove balls' and I shortly discovered that they'd spent it in the sweet-shop on the way (sweet-shops were for some reason always open on a Sunday though they were the only shops that were). After the singing we broke up into classes of about a dozen and the teachers gave us instruction on the Bible. Passages were read and expounded, after which we reassembled for the final hymn and prayer, the hymn nearly always being:

Now the day is over;
Night is drawing nigh
Shadows of the evening
Steal across the sky.[1]

The main object of it all was to familiarise us with the Bible. Considering our ages ranged from about four to ten the amount of misbehaviour wasn't great though we were pretty restless and fidgety. Very occasionally a real delinquent had to be punished by being made to stand on the platform beside the Superindenent but this was the worst that could be devised. Boys – it was always boys! – could hardly be expelled from a school whose raison d'etre was to bring them in, though one of the few who was ever singled out for platform exposure, named Reginald Jones, did in fact later land in a reformatory. He was in my class and I saw more of him out of class on the way home. I had a great way of getting into bad company.

It was while I attended Sunday School that I began to show traces of the cockney accent which so exercised my refined aunts and I suspect Mother may have had misgivings about my attendance there but no doubt she allowed herself to be overruled by Father. The church, its Boys' Brigade and its Sunday School had become a loyalty to which he felt himself dedicated; a way in which he could do some good. He was well aware that it was not a high-class place. The most educated people we came into contact with, apart from the ministers and their wives, were mostly schoolteachers. I sensed that Mother was aware of these limitations, as well as less involved in the activities, and although as a loyal wife she accepted them she will have been concerned about the long-term effect on me.

1 This, I find, is by a man for a change; both words and music are by 'Sabine Baring-Gould' (1834–1924), so still alive at that time) but how did he acquire such a strange name? Even stranger was that of J.B. Dykes (1823–76), composer of 'Fierce raged the tempest'; his middle name was Bacchus! What, in the year 1823, can have suggested such a remarkably un-Christian name for a boy?

It was characteristic of Father, however, to ensure that I didn't grow up to be a little snob and knew something of the working classes at first hand. I was conscious of differences and noticed that once, when the mother of one of our maids came to the back door to see Mother, she'd felt embarrassed at being shown into the drawing-room, but I wasn't allowed to be superior. Thanks to both Sunday School and the Boys' Brigade I got to know some of them quite well, and as human beings and not as if in another category of humanity. I learnt to talk to them without self-consciousness and wasn't disconcerted by them, and it was Father's straightforward, egalitarian manner towards them which showed me the way, though there were other influences too.

Around the time when I first attended Sunday School, and so must have been about four, Nellie, our maid, one day had a message to deliver to a Mrs Stoneham, one of the teachers, a working-class widow who lived in Waterloo Road, one of Romford's poorest streets. I went with her, for my afternoon walk, and in due course we entered a dingy, smelly garret with several small children hopping about. While Nellie was talking to Mrs Stoneham one of them came up and started touching me but I was repelled by his smell and pushed him away saying 'Go away, dirty!'. At this there was an outcry from the grown-ups. I was rebuked by Nellie for such behaviour while Mrs Stoneham explained that this was a 'little *poor* boy!'. I cried, of course, but was appeased with a piece of bread and marmalade which Mrs Stoneham spread with the back of the spoon, but I certainly picked up an appreciation of 'poverty' and the message that it behoved lucky people like me not to be disdainful.

By the time I had much to do with the BB, as it was often called, I was about eleven or twelve, and although Father was its Captain he didn't urge me to join it as I had homework to do. I was sometimes conscripted to play the piano for some of their 'drill' and got talking to them afterwards but I was also included in their annual camping holiday at Little Holland, just outside Clacton-on-sea and so got to know some of them fairly well. Although nearly all working-class most of the boys had parents who took their upbringing seriously and in this sense came from 'good' homes but there were one or two exceptions. One, in particular, who was in my tent, was a natural oaf; not ill-natured but of a crude, unambitious simplicity that seemed incapable of aspiring to anything else. I'd seen him once from the train during one of its typical waits outside Romford station, mucking oafishly about with another fellow, and I gathered he lived with an 'Aunty' who found him an encumbrance.

The other boys used to rag him a bit and of course I took my cue from them. I also used to swank wherever possible, to show off my superior education, and one evening in the tent, just before Lights Out, he made some remark which drew a scathing reply from me. After a while I suddenly realised he was crying – a boy of *his* age! – and he then burst out with 'You've spoilt my 'oliday, you 'ave!'. He'd looked forward to this, for him, most exceptional holiday and here was I, a conceited little show-off – and the Captain's son to boot – making him feel inferior. I felt so seared I hadn't a word to say in reply. Jack Saunter, the head of the tent, wanting to make me feel better about it, said 'Never mind, Bryson. Let's all go to sleep' but sleep, in my case, was a long time coming. I wondered if I ought to apologize but the next morning he seemed quite normal again and I couldn't think what to say so I said nothing, but the scar remained.

The camp lasted a week or ten days; long enough for some of the younger boys to feel homesick, and when we returned to Romford there were several mothers waiting to greet them on the platform. Most of the boys had reached the age when it was regarded as childish to be kissed and I was therefore the more struck when one of them, named Lillywhite, was greeted by his Mum with ''ullo Ducks!' and a smacking kiss. I could tell he felt self-conscious about being seen thus embraced but he was clearly glad about the embrace itself, and I was more alert to it after the searing moment with the oaf – who had no one to greet him.

Some time later another of the boys, having earned good marks at school and no doubt having aspiring parents, had applied to the local branch of Barclay's Bank for a white-collar job and given Father's name as a referee. At his initial intereview the Manager had said 'You're just the type of young man we're looking for' and given him a form to fill in. The completed form, however, revealed that his father was a house-painter and at this the Manager had said that in that case, he was sorry, but it was quite impossible to accept him. The poor boy wrote to Father reporting all this and his letter included the words 'I cannot tell you how I felt'. Father showed me the letter, evidently wanting me to appreciate how the world worked, and again the message was not lost on me, not the least part of it being his desire that I should know.

For much of my early life 'Father' was almost the same category as 'God' and I feared him and revered him accordingly. His example was as impressive as his words, indeed even more so as he was not greatly given to uttering moral injunctions. His usual method, when faced with the need for something like it, was to quote, and it was not necessarily a biblical quote; his favourite expressions came from the most diverse sources. One was 'The road to hell is paved with good intentions' but another, even more thought-provoking, was 'Men are usually right in what they assert and wrong in what they deny' (which I think comes from John Stuart Mill). More to be expected were ones from Burns, notably 'Man's inhumanity to man', and a particular favourite was 'And each the other's welfare kindly spiers' from 'The Cottar's Saturday Night' which reminded him of Scotland in his boyhood. He was an immensely hard worker and when reproached by Mama for overdoing it would say 'Better to wear out than rust out', a maxim which was also addressed to me if I complained that something was hard work. If I was perfunctory or slap-dash about something I was likely to get 'Whatsoever thy hand findeth to do, do it with thy might', or else the more up-to-date version 'If a thing's worth doing it's worth doing properly'. His declared aim in life, and one which he urged on me, was 'to do something to justify your existence' and 'to leave the world a better place than you found it'. At quite a different level, at the meal table when we had salad, he would quote Sydney Smith's:

> Let onion atoms lurk within the bowl
> And, scarce suspected, animate the whole.

In his homilies to the Boys' Brigade – and my attendance at the camp enabled me to hear him in the role of preacher – he was more direct and spoke in quiet, persuasive tones without a trace of sermonising. In the one I recall best he quoted 'To thine own self be true' and its main theme was that one shouldn't excuse oneself present wrongdoing with the thought that one would repent and make amends later, in fact he deprecated death-bed repentance altogether, and disapproval of Roman Catholic practices was implied. It was one of his few prejudices and he sometimes backed it with another quote from Mill: 'The idea creates the organisation and the organisation kills the idea', but he wasn't so bigoted as to hold it against persons; one of his chief colleagues at the office, almost a buddy, was a Catholic.

It was characteristic of him to have formed a company of the Boys Brigade, an organisation founded, he told me, in Glasgow (in 1883) by a man named Alexander Smith, with a view to getting potential delinquents off the streets, providing them with a simple uniform and some drill, both in the way of marching and gymnastics, with the occasional march through the town to show themselves off to the public and give them something to be proud of. A given company of it was always attached to a church, and 'Bible Class' was one of its activities. It went without saying, therefore, that the boys frequently found themselves singing hymns, many of them – as also at Sunday School and even in Church – full of military imagery. Not only the famous 'Onward, Christian soldiers, Marching as to war', but a whole armoury of others:

> Stand up, stand up for Jesus!
> Ye soldiers of the cross . . .

This day the noise of battle,
    The next the victor's song. (1858)

Brightly gleams our banner,
    Pointing to the sky,
Waving on Christ's soldiers
    To their home on high.
(1869, tune also by Sullivan)

Sound the battle-cry,
See, the foe is nigh.
Hold you standard high
    For the Lord. (1869)

These were likewise Victorian survivals, reflecting the Muscular Christianity that had been influential when Father was a young man. To be a Christian didn't mean to be a sissy, hence his cold baths and similar stoical practices.[2] War, in fact, had almost acquired a good image through being associated with Good Causes, and so formed an unconscious element in the cheering which hailed the departure of drafts of soldiers to the front. The image was still being used by the Evangelists in the 1920s. I was once taken, rather unwillingly, to one of their meetings where it was essential not only to have one's Bible but, at a certain point, to tuck it under one's arm. We then sang:

2 Their prorotype seems to have been the work of the pre-Victorian Bishop Heber who followed up the success of 'Greenland's icy mountains' (1819 – four years after that Famous Victory, the Battle of Waterloo) with another in 1827:

The son of God goes forth to war
    A kingly crown to gain.
His blood-red banner streams afar.
    Who follows in his train?

which was still being a success in my time. If the copyright laws of those days had been what they are for modern pop-stars, some of those hymn-writers would have become millionaires.

Draw you swords! Draw your swords!
For the battle is the Lord's.
Lean on him. Lean on him, and
Draw · your · swords!

and on the word 'draw' we had to whip the Bibles out from under our arms and brandish them in the air. The Bible was a sword.

The Evangelists, preoccupied with their 2000-year-old 'good news', had clearly given little thought to the dated ineptitude of the metaphor but it was during the 1910s, thanks to that war which was their main feature, that religious doubt extended from the thinking few to all classes. One would hear people asking 'How could God be good if he let such a disaster happen?' It could be answered by pointing out that the war was Man's doing, not God's; it was due to the abuse of Man's God-given faculties but they could be forgiven for having thought otherwise; up to Victorian times, and beyond, God's omnipotence was almost unquestioned. The second line of that Litany: 'Eternal Father strong to save' was 'Whose arm doth bind the restless wave'. If He controlled the waters to this extent He could have prevented the death of all those sailors had He wanted. Once one started thinking about the nature of 'God' there were other disturbing thoughts to hand. He might have made all things bright and beautiful but He'd also created 'Nature red in tooth and claw'. All creatures, great and small alike, fed on lesser creatures. This was apparently part of the set-up, God's Creation. I heard arguments of this sort being used by Pen's fiance who, having quarrelled with his parents' Evangelism, found it necessary to arm himself with arguments against religion and would have heated discussions with our family over the meal-table, meanwhile feasting on roast lamb.

Father was clear-headed enough to see the force of such arguments but they were not enough to break a lifetime's habit of going to church. He and many others consoled themselves with hymns which entertained 'honest doubt', notably one taken from Tennyson's 'In Memoriam':

Strong Son of God, immortal Love,
Whom we, who have not seen thy face,
By faith and faith alone embrace,
Believing where we cannot prove. (1833)

This was a far cry from Watts's apocalyptic certainties. It was sung to a tune by John Bacchus Dykes and had been in the hymnbook all the time but it was only after the war that I heard it sung. It was a sign of changed times.

Post-War Celebrations

The end of the war, though it often involved much agonised looking back, did at least allow some looking forward. There was a future of some sort ahead and the sensible thing was to make the best of it, indeed for many, to try to improve on the past. Mother and Father, like most Liberals, became strong supporters of the League of Nations and of the Union which promoted support for it. I was often sent to deliver circulars and the like to its various members, thereby discovering hitherto unknown corners of Romford, notably the further reaches of Mawney Road where it petered out into fields. In my earliest teens I studied the League's propaganda and was entirely persuaded by it, in fact became a strong supporter of it myself until Hitler's activities made it pointless.

In the immediate post-war aftermath there were also follow-ups of wartime acquaintance. During it, the Artists' Rifles had had a camp at Gidea Park (Wilfred Owen had been stationed there) and young men from it had often been invited to our house for a Pleasant Sunday Afternoon, or Evening, bringing their music. With the war over they would re-appear, bringing their parents to introduce them to the people who'd so kindly taken an interest in their sons during that terrible time. One of them – who brought his mother in the side-car of his motor-cycle – was unintentionally the occasion for Pen's marriage into the evangelistic family previously mentioned.

One day we were told that a young man who was a distant Canadian cousin would be coming, Mother having been asked to get in touch with him after his demobilisation and on his way back to Canada. The news rather excited us; these young soldiers were usually very kind to us but poor Roy, when he appeared, was silent and morose and for most of the time sat wordless on the sofa. After he'd gone Mother said she believed he was suffering from 'shellshock'. Out in the town Disabled Soldiers became a common sight and one day there was a man with two pegs for legs who kept himself propped up with a stick and, in a tremendous tenor voice, sang 'I'm for ever blowing bubbles' at the side of South Street. He got what seemed to me a great many pennies in his upturned cap and it didn't occur to me to wonder how he'd fare thereafter, or what became of the many without a singing voice. At the Maypole Dairies, where one day we'd heard one of the girls call out 'Mr Busby. Got any change?', and laughed among ourselves afterwards at such a funny name, we shortly found that Mr Busby, the boss, was no longer there; he'd diedd, almost overnight, in the 'flu epidemic'. Several years later, when we'd moved to Surrey, we saw the husband of a young neighbour in a wheel-chair and learnt that he'd been 'gassed'. His face was grey and he spent most of his time sitting silent in the sun. Then, within a year or two, he died, about seven years after the war.

For employed survivors, however, the end of food shortages meant a resumption of the Edwardian invitations to afternoon tea favoured by ladies of that period. We children were not usually present but we knew when they were going to take place as Mother would spend the morning cooking scones and cakes. Sometimes I was required to pass cups and plates and offer scones and cakes with my best party manners on but most often the ladies had their chin-wag without the presence of little pitchers and only on the point of their departure were we called in to say a polite 'How d'ye do'. It could be instructive none the less; the ladies varied considerably and the ways of some of them were in striking contrast to Mother's; one or two of them were very voluble and tallked in exaggerated ways which we enjoyed imitating after they'd gone.

Naturally there were return invitations and in special cases we might be in on those. One frosty day in early 1919 we accompanied Mother to 'town', crossed from Liverpool Street to Broad Street and took the North London line to Oakleigh Park, changing at Finsbury Park. This was where the Evangelists lived, the wealthiest house I'd ever been into. The daughter of the house, who was the same age as Pen, had a large 'nursery with a huge dolls' house that you could *walk into*! and many expensive toys lying about. Other people's houses could be as arresting as their ways of talking and behaving and this one, with diverse members of the family dispersed about it, and with servants emerging from behind green-baize doors, had the enviable air of a 'going concern', even though I knew little of the details. One detail which particularly arrested me was the presence of large framed Bible texts in conspicuous positions on the walls. One was informed, in ornate coloured lettering, that 'AS FOR ME AND MY HOUSE, WE WILL SERVE THE LORD'.

As for tea, I'd never seen such a spread. We sat at a huge table and the number of jams, scones, cakes and biscuits was unparalleled in my experience. The lady of the house, mother of four children, let it be known that she fully understood a desire to sample them all and at one point, seeing my plate empty, asked me what I'd like next. I was reduced to silence and then had to explain that I didn't know the name of the particular goodie I had my eye on, so she said 'Point to it'. When I did so she said, 'O, you mean almond fingers!' and a silver cakedish containing almond fingers on a doily was handed in my direction. This special dispensation from the rule that it was 'rude to point' earned her a very good mark in my estimation.

She earned another when, after tea, we returned to the huge drawing-room and played musical chairs while she played Blake's Grand March at the grand piano. I liked it so much that I enquired the name of it and, back in Romford, asked Madame Snell if I could have it as a piece. She told me to get a copy from our local music shop who produced a pre-War edition costing sixpence (2 pence). This was wonderfully cheap – I'd expected to pay two shillings – and it was duly added to my repertory. It proved a great deal easier than 'Coriolanus', as well as more popular with audiences. Uncle John was continually asking me to play it and sometimes marched to it while I did so, whereas my version of Coriolanus left him quite unmoved.

A lady who frequently came to tea, and to whose house further up Western Road we were counter-invited, was Mrs Gibson and she was not merely voluble, she was positively melodramatic and wore clothes to match, particularly heliotrope and purple, gesturing freely to enhance her talk while we watched transfixed. On one occasion she was full of her eldest daughter, Christine, who was studying to be a doctor (an exceptional career for a girl in those days) and had apparently done very well in a recent exam. When she was on the point of leaving Mother said something polite to the effect that she was glad Christine was getting on so well at which Mrs Gibson turned in the doorway, held up a stiffened forearm to demonstrate iron determination, and wagged it in Mother's face saying 'She's got the metal in her, Mrs Gerrard'. Although I could identify iron, copper and brass I hadn't fully grasped the meaning of the generic word 'metal' and this startling demonstration suddenly suggested it. It was also prize material for imitation when next we came to play charades.

The Gibsons were in a different category from the rest of our acquaintance, partly because they had no connection with the church. Mr and Mrs Gibson both spoke with strong Scottish accents and I think this was the chief reason we knew them (Scots tend to hang together) though there was also the fact that they had five children of whom the middle ones were about our ages and lived only about 100 yards up the road. Mr Gibson worked in the City and was something of a go-getter and money-maker. His interests didn't include gardening and their front garden was a choked wilderness of overgrown berberis. The house was still there in 1982 and by that time the jungle had been cleared to make room for a car but it wasn't the first car to be owned at that house. Having evidently done all right during the war Mr Gibson decided to celebrate its end by buying a secondhand Oldsmobile and on Boxing Day, 1918, word was sent round to our house asking if I'd like to go with them on a trip to Southend-on-Sea for the day. I needed no urging. A ride in a car was as exciting as a ride in a train and good deal more exceptional. It was stressed that I should wrap up well, it being a frosty day.

That outing was a brief reversion to the *status quo ante bellum* though few other ex-Edwardians were making similar trips. The car had a canvas roof and its sides were open so that wrapping up well was indeed desirable; we had rugs galore and Mrs Gibson wore a fur coat. Before we started I was allowed to sound the horn, or rather to try to, only to find that my hand was too small to squeeze the black rubber bulb quickly enough to produce any sound. There was also a claxon with a metal-knobbed plunger which one thrust down into its box, thus producing an ugly great blurt but having been allowed to do it once I was discouraged from repeating it. Mr Gibson cranked up the engine, took the driver's seat and announced 'I'll drive ye at fifty mile an hour' but we knew him to be a bit of a boaster and were not apprehensive. Tommy, his eldest son, sat next to him and at one point, along a fairly straight stretch of gritty road, drew our attention to the speedometer; we were doing 'Thirty miles an hour!'.

The road was familiar as far as Hornchurch but after that it was unknown country even to Mr Gibson, the car being such a recent acquisition. We passed through quiet Essex villages and I noticed the names of Horndon and Laidon on signposts (Basildon didn't then exist), but these directed one to the next village or villages and we had to stop more than once to ask some solitary pedestrian the way. He – or in one case she – seldom seemed to know; they could only tell us about places fairly close at hand. There was no accepted through road and we didn't find a signpost pointing to Southend-on-Sea until we got within two or three miles of it. Tommy agreed with his father that for future journies they must get a map without delay and study it in advance.

Southend, when we finally reached it, was as dead as might have been expected on a Boxing Day. Demobilisation had evidently not taken place on any scale, or else the recently returned 'ex-soldiers' were recovering quietly at home; they certainly weren't out on the streets. I was very disappointed that the pier, which we'd visited once in sunnier circumstances and which was 'a mile long!' and had a tram along it, was closed. The pubs seemed to be open but we didn't go into one. Instead we ate our sandwiches in the car on the esplanade, washing them down with tea from Mrs Gibson's thermos flask.

How long it had taken us to get there was not a matter to which I'd given much thought but I gathered the journey was about 'thirty miles' so having finished our picnic on the esplanade we started back and the return journey took even longer. Night fell long before we were home and the car's lights had to be lit. This meant getting out of the car – we all got out to 'stretch our legs' – and Mr Gibson, taking a box of matches to the great gig-lamps which were the 'headlights' while we all watched. First he had to turn a little tap in the upper compartment which contained water, thus letting water drip onto the 'calcium carbide' in the lower compartment. This generated 'acetylene gas' of which the strange acrid smell drifted over to us, then he opened the glass door in front of the lamp, applied a lighted match to the burner and an incandescent blade of white flame spurted therefrom. We were then invited to bob down to a level where we could see it reflected in the mirror behind it and lo and behold! a dazzling bright headlight!

In spite of headlights, however, finding our way was no easier than it had been on the outward journey and there were fewer people about to ask. At least once we took a wrong turning, and had to come back. It must have been pretty late when we finally reached Western Road but I had no thought for such details. It had been a unique experience. Nothing quite like it would ever happen again. The Edwardian age was over.

The same applied to many things around this time. With increasing speed the old order yielded place to new. The rural quietness of Petit's Lane with its blackberry hedges was rudely cut across by the 'Southend Arterial Road' (Eastern Avenue). Mr Mann's fields, where I'd taken part in that play of Tolstoy's, was built over so that the view across the lake from Raphael Park was no longer of fields but of houses. Stewards

Manor, the sixteenth-century home of Francis Quarles at the corner of Western Road and South Street, was rased to the ground to make room for shops and a cinema. A similar fate overtook 'Payne's Fields' between Junction Road and Balgore's Lane which, via a footpath from Junction Road, had been the nearest place for a walk or a picnic, as well as the usual place where Hugh Gibson and I went catching butterflies – Small Heaths, Small Coppers, Meadow Browns, Wall Browns . . . it had been in a patch of thistles near the railway line that I'd caught that Bath White. From the train between Romford and Chadwell Heath could be seen signs of extensive building and I learnt that this was a new housing estate: 'Becontree Heath'. Until then the view had been chiefly of London's market gardens and recalled a land where I'd once gone cycling with a schoolfriend who lived in Goodmayes.

The return of the railways to normal meant that, at last, one could get chocolate from the automatic machines on the stations; flat little slabs of Nestle's Swiss Milk in silver paper with an outside wrapping of vermilion paper. One could also get cigarettes; two Woodbines or one Churchman for a penny (a twelfth of a shilling) but an expensive way to buy them. If one had the nerve one could get a paper packet of five Woodbines or Weights from the tobacconist for 2d. but there was always the risk of his saying you were too young and refusing to sell. The machine obviated this hazard and smoking was another piece of schoolboy wickedness that could be indulged when one got 'an empty'. Peace-time also made it possible for Father to have his own long-awaited celebration: a holiday in Scotland.

Scotland

Father's ancestors came from Buchan, in the north of Aberdeenshire, and throughout his life he retained a deep loyalty towards the land of his fathers. He almost felt he'd been robbed of his birthright through having been born in Market Deeping, Lincolnshire. At one period of his childhood, he told us, he'd spent a year in New Aberdour and got to know the place and its people, many of them relatives, and was still in correspondence with several of them. Nothing more natural, therefore, that with the war out of the way and money in the bank, it should be chosen for our holiday in 1919 and this meant the exciting prospect of pistoning tremendously through the night on the Great Northern, the Northern-Eastern and the North British to 'Scotland'.

We had in fact been once before the war – it must have been in 1913 – but, not yet three, I had only the most patchy recollections of it though such vignettes as I retained had that magical, almost mythological quality: eating oatmeal porridge with a 'bowlie' (to rhyme with Cowley) of milk at the side of our plates; drinking a cup of milk still warm from the cow; climbing a ladder in a farm building and finding a group of village youths there on a Sabbath afternoon one of whom picked me up and held me up-side-down over the trap door so that I was terrified, the more so as I couldn't understand a word of their local 'Doric'; being taken to see 'the hermit' who lived in a cave a little way up the rocky coast. We saw him only from a distance and he seemed a pretty ragged spectacle with an immensely long beard. What he lived on and whether he continued to live in that cold and stormy cave throughout the winter I failed to ask but I was conscious of a very strange phenomenon from Father's way of talking about it.

By the time of this second visit, when I was rising nine, I was all set to notice every detail of the railway aspect of the journey and Father was full of information about it but apart from the fact that it was a hot August night at Kings Cross I was less conscious of the details of departure then from Euston three years previously. In the bosom of the family I felt more at ease than in the company of Grannie and Aunt Catherine and sleep came easily. A smell associated with it was a compound of Worcester Permaine apples, ham sandwiches, hard-boiled eggs – a 'picnic' in the train was part of the excitement – and the leather of Father's Gladstone bag. After that I knew no more until we were drawing in Princes Street, Edinburgh, in the early morning and in another country, the magic carpet having performed one of its most advanced feats. During the long wait in the station another smell assailed our nostrils; a compound of coalsmoke, fish, oranges and other fruit and vegetables. All long distance haulage was by rail and the platforms of big stations that handled food-traffic smelt like Covent Garden market. (The middle platforms of the old Euston station retained that smell to the end.)

No details escaped me when we at last puffed northward, still in the early morning magic: the Forth Bridge, 'over a mile long!' and still regarded by Father as one of the seven wonders of the world; the Tay Bridge, with the still visible remains of the one that had blown down; breakfast of kippers and toast and tea in the restaurant of Aberdeen station with its bentwood chairs and a coatstand of curling bentwood antlers; and finally the last lap of the Great North of Scotland Railway. Despite its high-sounding name this was no East Coast Express; it started as a typical Victorian 'tram' and had hardly pulled out of Aberdeen station when it stopped at 'Schoolhill' on the other side of Union Street, followed in quick succession by Kittybrewster, Woodside and Bucksburn, followed shortly by Dyce Junction. After that we were on single track and Father drew our attention to the system for ensuring that only one train could be on a given stretch of line at a time; as the train embarked on it the signalman held out the 'token', a wallet attached to a hoop through which the driver or stoker looped his arm as he passed; so long as it was in their possession they could chuff along the stretch without misgiving. On reaching the next station we saw the signalman there waiting with his arm outstretched to receive it back in readiness for the next train going in the opposite direction.

Father's excitement at being once again on what was, for him, almost sacred ground communicated itself to me, though I needed little encouragement to respond. When we were nearing Fraserburgh he pointed out 'the Hill o' Mormond', a long low tawny-coloured mound with a silent, sinister-seeming presence. It was a sign that we were 'nearly there'. The little terminus of Fraserburgh smelt strongly of fish but we wasted no time there; there was still a last lap of journey by road in a sort of hackney-cab – in 1913 it had been horse-drawn – which covered the last ten miles to New Aberdour, finally arriving at the 'Commercial Hotel' where Mr Fraser, the proprietor, was awaiting us. Facing one, as one entered, was a large mirror with 'India Pale Ale' painted on it in ornamental letters. I wondered what Pale Ale had to do with India and guessed there must be some connection with Ind Coope who had a brewery at Romford. On the right was a sign: 'Bar'; I was actually entering a pub, and with full parental approval! but we turned left and went upstairs where we were shown to comfortable bedrooms. The dining-room too was upstairs and at every meal there was a large basket of home-made oatcakes and unlimited butter. For breakfast we had boiled eggs with horn egg-spoons, and wooden egg-cups.

Out in the village there was a new smell: peatsmoke, a much more romantic smell than coalsmoke – the railway was now far away. A fine summer morning can still remind me of that clean, clear summer-holiday air with its drift of peatsmoke and baking oatcakes. In the banks of the long road down to the sea there were harebells – Scottish bluebells – and then at last there was the sea itself, first the Broad Shore and then, on the other side of a little headland, the Boat Shore where we used to bathe. Bathing was supposed to be a rapturous experience yet the water was infernally cold and even a short spell of splashing about in it was likely to produce 'the shivers', that uncontrollable trembling of goose-fleshy limbs which took a long time to wear off, even after one was dressed. Father didn't deny that the water was cold but it was apparently 'good for you' to plunge bravely in and then to feel the nice warm glow when you came out.

This was partly the Muscular Christian speaking, though it was also loyalty to his beloved Aberdour which was beyond criticism. Having been toughened up himself as a child he reckoned I ought to have the same treatment, and part of me was quite content to undergo it. For me, too, it was almost sacred ground; it was the home of my ancestors. One place of pilgrimage was the churchyard by the sea with its old ruined church. It was still used as the local burying-ground and I at once noticed a new gravestone of black granite commemorating 'William Gerrard' in gold letters, Father's 'Uncle Willie' who'd been alive – though bed-ridden – at the time of the 1913 visit. Father pointed out earlier gravestones, and although no expert on dates I could appreciate that one which began with 17– was very early. The last stone we looked at, off which Father had to scrape the moss, commemorated 'John Gerard', with one r, whose date of birth was 16– . . . I didn't remember but as it was the last grave we looked at, and was surveyed in silence, it was presumably the earliest. (It has since set me wondering whether he was a Huguenot who escaped to Scotland after the Revocation of the Edict of Nantes. Scottish pronunciation would no doubt account for the name acquiring a double r in the course of time.)

Close by the churchyard was a small, empty roofless building which Father told us had formerly been the school-house. The schoolmaster had lived there and the children paid their fees in kind, bringing gifts of oatmeal and the like. In the 1850s his own mother had been one of the pupils, walking the several miles daily to and from Cowford's farm which her father owned. A detail which intrigued me was that the children mostly went with bare feet, not because they were poverty-stricken, which they weren't, but simply to save unnecessary waste of good shoe leather; children's feet grow fast; they could graduate to shoes when they stopped growing. I too liked to go about with bare feet – anyway in summer – but was not encouraged to do so in Romford where it at once brought the stigma of poverty.

An outing one day was to Cuminestown, a village about a dozen miles away where Uncle Willie's widow still lived. This meant a journey by pony-and-trap across vast moorlands of purple heather. At one point the road ran straight ahead down into a valley and straight up the other side, and I exclaimed that on the further side it looked almost vertical. When we reached it it proved to be merely steep but, even so, too steep to expect the poor pony to haul all of us up it; we got out and walked alongside until we reached the top of the hill. I did so with fervour, out of sympathy for the pony, but was struck by the reminder that people who worked with and depended on animals developed an almost 'human' relationship with them and were always conscious of their needs – as the Romford cabmen had been of their horses.

I have no very clear recollection of the inside of 'Aunt Margaret's' house in Cuminestown – I think we were sent out to play while our seniors talked about the past – but I still possess a solid momento of it; her husband had been the village blacksmith but in addition was no mean carpenter and the chair on which I'm sitting at this moment was made by him. It is not at all the bent-wood type; far more solid and serviceable and with a quiet, almost eighteenth-century dignity about it. She left it to Father when she died, and when I first knew it, it had a horse-hair seat which pricked the underside of childish bare knees but it nevertheless brought with it the quiet security of those simple, self-dependent little houses in that remote countryside where people worked hard, wasted not and wanted not, and were less at the mercy of the booms and depressions that could afflict a wider world. Another legacy now in my possession is a grandfather clock made by 'Geo. Hardy, Old Deer'. Old Deer is another village, not much further off, and the clock was formerly at Cowfords Farm. It dates from c.1830 and is neither crude nor grandiose; it too has a certain eighteenth-century elegance and has since provoked the reflection that Scotland, further off from the Great Wen, addicted to education long before the Education Act of 1870, stirred by Burn's egalitarian reminder that 'A man's a man for a' that', and in any case having its own honour and dignity, retained much of the eighteenth century's sense of proportion long after Victorian tastes had driven it out further south. The clock still keeps perfect time – it can be fine-tuned despite the simplest of mechanisms – and stings out the hours to this house with a precision which half-charms, half-shames me. It is a reminder that the forefathers of those various hamlets were far from 'rude'. My great-grandfather had been the blacksmith of New Aberdour and between the strokes on the anvil had taught himself Latin and provided a home background which enabled his eldest son, my grandfather, to work his way to Aberdeen University and ultimately to become a veterinary surgeon.

What that background was like could be gleaned from further anecdotes reported by Father. A smithy, in such agricultural parts, was a centre where people from miles around would bring their horses and talk while waiting for them to be attended to; a place of gossip but not only gossip; they would report their problems and air their grievances, or disputes about land and tenure. My great-grandfather evidently acquired a reputation for giving sound advice in such matters, even, I gathered, being sometimes asked to adjudicate and give a decision. That they were considered just decisions was evidenced by the fact that he became known as 'Honest John Gerrard'; his counsel was regarded as detached and disinterested, and I feel sure he won't have charged for it, though I suppose a grateful client may sometimes have brought him a bag of oatmeal or a dozen eggs in the same way as the children paid their school fees. The Gerrards and the Galls – my paternal grandmother was a Gall – were apparently described locally as 'high-minded', a word which it was explained to me meant not 'stuck-up' but the opposite of 'petty'; having a broader vision than most. Understandably some of the women became schoolteachers, and not only the women; 'Uncle John Gall' (really my great-uncle) was Professor of Mathematics at Lucknow University. The Greek and Latin dictionaries to which I resort are inherited from him.

That I should have drunk all this in and remembered it was largely due, I think, to the fact that Father, with his beloved Scotland to stimulate him, was far more talkative than usual and a child's almost animal instinct for noting tones of voice in grown-ups tells them what grade of importance to give to what is being said. I don't recall that he enjoined me to be as good as my ancestors but he left me in no doubt that they were something to be proud of. Although by now, born and brought up in England, I mostly regard myself as an Englishman – and call myself a Londoner – I have never forgotten this yardstick by which to measure myself and despite often feeling a most unworthy inheritor it has been a permanent influence.

Another Scottish legacy is good husbandry. 'Waste not, want not' was instilled into us from the start, the more so as Mother and Father had both endured hard times when young though I fancy it would have happened anyway. The proverbial Scotsman was supposed to be parsimonious, indeed mingey, and there used to be innumerable jokes about him, most of them grossly exaggerated, but I never thought them more than moderately funny. It seemed to me common sense to make the most of your material and not to throw anything away unless you had to. It still does, and I am horrified at the extravagant way the 'never had it so good' generation will throw away perfectly good food, clothes, anything they've ceased immediately to want. I feel quite unrepentant at making a certain amount of food last for two meals, or saving up something because it might come in handy, and feel the greatest satisfaction when one day it does.

One Christmas Father gave Pen and me a jig-saw puzzle each; for her a map of England and for me of Scotland, the shape and size of the pieces being determined by the boundaries of the shires. He'd made them himself, getting paper maps of the two countries and a thin wooden board, sticking the former onto the latter and doing the rest with a fret-saw, including a box to contain the pieces. We were delighted, did the puzzles over and over again and as a result learnt the exact geography of the two countries. It was a geography lesson as well as a pleasure. Total cost: a few old pence. Money saved in this sort of way had contributed to his being able to afford the holiday in Scotland – and later the new house in Surrey.

'America'

The American 'explosion' which first began to manifest itself in a big way after the war is one of the major facts of twentieth-century history. It had in fact begun manifesting itself before the war – Debussy's 'Golliwog's Cake-walk' was written in 1908 – and a little reflection reveals that a lot of American material had been around our house for a long time without the fact of its 'American-ness' being appreciated. Pen had a copy of *Little Women* and of *What Katy did*, and when I reached the stage of devouring every book I came across I read both, sensing that their background was 'different' but not yet critical enough to ask myself what that difference was. We also had *Uncle Tom's Cabin* in a 'Told to the Children' abbreviated version and Mother told us about 'slavery' but I was chiefly conscious of an interesting – though awfully sad – story. 'Under the spreading chestnut tree' and 'The Children's Hour' – both in our poetry book at Miss Jones's – were likewise uncritically accepted. (Longfellow was in fact one of the most popular poets of the nineteenth century throughout Britain.) Around the time Miss Jones was making us aware of a traditional England with such carols as 'The holly and the ivy' and 'Here we come a-wassailing', the children of the Upper Sunday School sang a carol I hadn't heard before which seemed to touch a similar nerve, though it was a good many years before I discovered that 'We three kings of Orient' was written and composed by Dr J.H. Hopkins, Jr, Rector of Christ Church, Williamsport, Pennsylvania, c.1857. Just when I learnt that 'Stand up for Jesus' and 'Jesus bids us shine' were of American provenance I don't remember but the fact made little impression at the time. In our music cabinet there was a popular collection of songs called 'The Scottish Students' Song-book' which included 'Riding down from Bangor', 'John Brown's Body', 'Marching through Georgia', 'Camptown Races', and 'Juanita' as well as a section called 'Plantation Songs' with such famous numbers as 'Old Folks at home', 'Poor old Joe', and the rest, all of which were sung round the piano in a multitude of British homes besides ours and were almost counted part of the national repertory. As with hymns, people annexed what attracted them regardless of origin.

In the matter of literature people were likely to be more aware of American provenance but Prescott's 'Conquests' were regarded as classics, and Webster's English Dictionary was accepted (still is) as one of the most authoritative. Emerson, Poe, Hawthorn, Oliver Wendell Holmes, Whittier, and novels by Winston Churchill all figured in Father's bookcase. Walt Whitman, too, though less 'popular' than Longfellow, was clearly admired among the more discerning. Two choral works in which I later found myself singing: 'Delius', 'Sea Drift' (1903) and Vaughan Williams' 'Sea Symphony' (1910) are to Whitman's words. American influence was undoubtedly there, though just what that influence was is harder to assess.

It must have been around 1917 that a song which seemed to strike a new note was transmitted on the bush telegraph and in no time had everyone singing it. Earlier in the war we'd had 'Tipperary', 'Keep the home fires burning', 'There's a long, long trail' and others of an English music-hall type but this one had a fascinatingly different air:

> Good-byee,
> Don't cry-ee
> Wipe the tear,
> Baby dear,
> From your ey-ee.

and it was the word 'Baby' which arrested. Until then it had signified 'infant' but it was clear that this was not what was intended and I gathered from Nellie that it meant 'sweetheart' in America. Later in the song came 'I'll · be · tickled to death to go'. 'Tickled to death' was likewise an unfamiliar expression though it at once took on, even if used a little facetiously and self-consciously. The rhythm of the song was also a shade more pungent than we were used to; half-reminiscent of ragtime though its tempo was gentle. Behind both words and music, however, was their general tenor; it was one thing to urge one's tearful sweetheart to 'turn the dark cloud inside out till the boys come home', or to wait 'until the time that I'll be going down that long, long trail with you'; it was quite another to assert, with manifestly bogus bragadoccio, that one was tickled to death to go and finally depart with 'Cheerio, Chin-chin, Toodle-oo, Good-byee', though when talkies later came in I noticed that Americans put on a bold face for such occasions and hid their real feelings under a blatant jauntiness.

Once the war was over a much more thorough-going jauntiness not only became normal; it became the rage, and it was then that American popular music hit a war-ravaged Europe and took it by storm. At least, it took the younger generation by storm though it rather scandalised the older who were half-horrified by its all-too-pungent 'syncopated' rhythm and regarded it as 'vulgar'. (It was still scandalising Hitler a decade later and he tried to ban it). It may have been African in inspiration but 'America' got the credit/blame for it. It was the age of 'Bye, bye, blackbird', 'Avalon', 'Swannee', 'My blue heaven', *et al* and by that time the bush telegraph was finding increasing support from the gramophone. One day Pen startled the family by suddenly bursting out with:

Mar - gie,
I'm always thinking of you,
Mar - gie,
I'll tell the world I love you,
Don't · for - get · your
Promise to me.
I · have · got · a
Home and ring
And everything
And days are never blue.

But when all is said and done
There is really only one
And Margie, Margie
It's you.

(I've hardly given it a thought for sixty years but this trots our verbatim and the tune along with it.) Father was more than startled; he was half-shocked though he found it hard to say why. For my part I was amazed that Pen knew all the words (probably picked up from 'a girl at school') but one word in particular arrested: my old friend 'blue' with reference for days. From my understanding of it the days should have been always blue, i.e. heavenly. This was the beginning of a now familiar image of it as 'miserable', at all events when the context is American.

Then a Rhodesian cousin who'd won a Rhodes Scholarship to Oxford came to stay for a few days and electrified us by spanking out 'Chicago' at the piano. He was followed not long afterwards by Cousin Nesta from Scotland who demonstrated that the Scottish young were similarly 'with it' by giving us 'Dinah', 'Dardanella', 'Omaha' and others. The word 'electrified' might be applied to Father and Mother but the current was clearly too strong for them to feel happy about it. It was like being required, out of politeness, to swallow a dose of neat whiskey, a drink they never touched. Such music was summarily described as 'jazz' and as it became more familiar I noticed that Father was sometimes capable of responding to its sensational lilt but he gave the impression that he felt he ought not to; it was not so much vulgar as animal; it seemed to release impulses that ought to be kept under control.

Similar uncertainty coloured their attitude to the cinema, and this was the moment when American films made their first sensational impact. They didn't exactly disapprove of it – Mother taking us to the 'Four Horseman' was evidence – but for the most part they didn't encourage it. Mrs Gibson – characteristically – had once persuaded Mother to accompany her to the Victory Palace to see 'Tarzan of the Apes' but this was clearly not Mother's line of country and she didn't feel it would have been particularly improving for us. The working classes, however, had no such inhibitions and Nellie, and Miss Colebrook, the chief of the Croydon seamstresses, would excitedly recount 'episodes' of such serials as 'The Perils of Pauline' and 'Miracles of the Jungle'. The lurid posters outside the cinemas announced these and others as 'melodramas' and it was an accurate description. It is little wonder if the more discerning were somewhat contemptuous of the cinema of that time.

Not so myself, however. I went crazy about it and seized every opportunity of going. The price of the cheapest seats was 3d (1p in current terms) and once or twice I stole this amount out of a drawer – supposed to be secret – where Father sometimes put the collection money from Sunday School. When I hadn't got any money I used to hang about outside the push-bar doors which guarded the rear exit of the Victory Palace and listen to the 'orchestra' just inside them. I then discovered that these doors didn't always close automatically when people came out of them so that I could peer in and watch the screen sideways on. Once, when one of the usherettes found me there, and as the programme was nearly over she told me to come in and sit in the front row.

It was almost immaterial to me what the film was about, nor was the Forbidden Fruit aspect very important; it was chiefly the phenomenon of Moving Pictures which entranced me. There, high in the wall at the back of the hall, was a little window behind which was what I knew to be a 'projector', and an expanding beam of light with cigarette smoke rising through it traversed the whole length of the hall to reveal unfamiliar scenes magically in motion. The fact that it always seemed to be raining hard or that people moved with unnatural speed, didn't worry me in the slightest and I used to like it when, for a moonlight scene, the screen turned blue, or, for a fire, red. The captions, too, would come out with unfamiliar expressions such as 'Say, Bo', or the adjective 'swell' to mean very nice. I saved up my money, largely by going without lunch – I was now at the City of London School – and one day bought a cheap projector at Gamages in High

Holborn. It was really a ghastly apparatus but I saw only its good points. The film smelt strongly of cellulose and as it was highly inflammable Father forbade me to use it in the house. Projections therefore took place in the coal-shed, where it was dark, with invited friends to share the treat whenever possible.

The apotheosis of this movie-mania was represented by the Ilford Super Cinema whose construction I observed daily from the train, sometimes breaking the journey at Ilford to inspect its progress more closely. In due course it was formally opened and thereafter I frequently crossed its almost sacred threshold. It had 'marble' floors and pillars; two ticket offices, one on each side of the main entrance, with mechanised ticket-dispensers responding to the girls' taps on the knobs below; and further into its vast marble foyer there was a 'soda fountain'. It was far more deserving of the name of 'palace' than our Victory Palace at Romford with its corrugated iron roof, and no doubt this was a large part of its attraction; for the working classes in particular it was a more significant building than they'd formerly felt entitled to enter; now for a few pence they could do so and feel it to be their right. It also had a smell of its own which I find it hard to describe, or even to remember very exactly, but which was traceable to the synthetic 'June' scent sprayed with spray-guns by the usherettes from time to time. In the days before ventilation became efficient, halls with no windows acquired a strong 'unventilated' atmosphere, manifestly unhealthy, and the Victory Palace was a prize example. It may well have been one reason why my parents didn't encourage visits. No doubt the 'June' was more camouflage than cure but for me it was the smell of 'America'. Within its bouquet I saw the 'Four Horsemen' – for the second and third time – 'Under Two Flags', 'Way Down East', 'The Blue Lagoon' and others and failed to see 'The Birth of a Nation' and 'Intolerance'. Charlie Chaplin was reckoned to be compulsory viewing but for some reason I didn't find him very funny – too exaggerated – and preferred such comedians as Buster Keaton, Larry Simon and Harold Lloyd.

Quite independently, in 1920, 'America' was much more consciously introduced to us at church. It was the tercentenary of the Pilgrim Fathers who'd crossed the Atlantic in the 'Speedwell' and the 'Mayflower' in 1620 and founded the Plymouth Colony in Massachusetts, and the Congregational Church celebrated this in quite a big way. A special choir of children was formed for it and we rehearsed unfamiliar 'hymns' on specially printed hymn sheets. One was Julia Ward Howe's 'Battle Hymn of the Republic':

> Mine eyes have seen the glory
>   of the coming of the Lord;
> He is trampling out the vintage where the
>   grapes of wrath are stored.

Father told me that it was usually sung to the tune of 'John Brown's Body' but in the post-war period this was evidently deemed too martial and we had another, much more 'reverent' tune to sing (still largely retrievable). The same applied to:

> A ship went over the harbour-bar
>   Out into the open sea.
> She carried no . . . (was it 'war guns'?)
>   . . . at her side,
>   She flaunted no war flag in her pride,
>   She set her stem to the evening tide
>   And away to the west went she.

to the tempo of a leisurely six-eight, no doubt to suggest the rocking of sailing-ships on the waves.

The climax of the proceedings was an address by Mrs . . . memory again lets me down though the name might come unbidden given a chance prompting. We had no difficulty in understanding her but were really more interested in how she spoke than in what she had to say. Most of the time she was addressing the grown-up congregation while we choir-children sat behind her just below the pulpit but at one point she spoke about how much more vivid a child's memory is than a grown-up's and illustrated her point by picking up a large writing-pad and scribbling two wiggly lines across it; one very bold, the other very faint, and then held it up for the congregation to see. Having done so she didn't forget that we couldn't see it and turned round, holding it up for our benefit and saying 'I'm afRaid id isn'd a veRy beaudiful pictuRe, children', thereby giving an unconscious illustration of the point of her picture; as almost the first words I ever heard an American utter they got themselves remembered, especially those burred *r*s and turning *t* into a *d* when it came before vowels. We had to wait until talkies came in, some ten years later, before such speech became familiar.

We were then invited to believe that this was the way that we ourselves talked in the seventeenth century; that Americans had preserved intact 'Elizabethan' habits of speech. 'Evidence' was produced in the shape of words which were still used in the States but were obsolete in Britain, such as 'deck' for a 'pack' of cards, or 'honey' as a term of endearment. Even at the age of twenty or so I found it difficult to persuade myself that Shakespeare's way of talking would have much resembled that of Al Johnson or Clara Bow, and it didn't take long to work out that, quite apart from the Pilgrim Fathers having regional accents, habits of speech are continually changing and in two such different countries they would be likely to change in different directions. Even at the age of nine I was conscious of some growing apart.

The proceedings ended with John Bunyan's 'Who would true valour see' (or should I now write 'valor'?), a hymn which we held in common, and I feel sure that much will have been said about the close American connections that had existed at the religious level ever since 1620, barely interrupted by the War of Independence. The Dissenting churches in particular had been conscious of a special relationship and many at the British end had backed George Washington at that time. The churches were still aware of shared values and I feel sure that it was this early awareness that has tended to make me pro-American enough to feel indignant, rather than hostile, when the likes of Joe McCarthy, or Nixon, or Reagan betray her principles. They let 'us' down.

There were other aspects of growing apart of which Mrs . . . herself may only have been dimly aware in 1920, and we British even less so. We were imagining an America that no longer existed, forgetting – in so far as we were conscious of it – that great tide of emigration around the turn of the century which within two decades flooded the US with fourteen million newcomers, mostly from Eastern and Southern Europe, the former supplying the 'Moguls' of the cinema and 'Hollywood', the latter 'the Godfather' – or his antecedents – and 'Gangsterism'. These hit the Europe of the 1920s far more forcibly than ideas about Equality and even those, though Nonconformist values provided fertile ground for them, had been sparked off much more by Lafayette and French Revolutionary – and to some extend anti-British – notions of *Liberté, Egalité, Fraternité*. As for the language, increasingly since that time we have had to put up with hearing immigrant German-speakers use our language as if it were their own and say 'make' when they should say 'do', or call crochets and quavers 'quarter notes' and 'eighth notes'. 'Hopefully', that literal translation of the German *hoffentlich*, is in the same category but, like 'tickled to death' six or seven decades ago, and a hundred other expressions since, has tended to take on over here. During the 1939–45 war, when Americans of all levels of education came to Europe by the thousand, I one day felt a special relationship with a Sicilian I talked to in Catania; we felt ourselves fellow-Europeans by reaction to them; their ways were not our ways . . .

A Populous and Smoky City

Hell is a city much like London –
  A populous and smoky city;
There are all sorts of people undone,
And there is little or no fun done;
  Small justice shown and still less pity.

Shelley, 'Peter Bell the Third'

Some twenty years ago I read a book called 'John Bull's Schooldays'; a symposium of accounts of their schooldays by a diversity of men who'd since become well-known, and was struck by the number who looked back with dislike, or at best amused derision; a time in their lives they were glad to leave behind them. Two, however, were conspicuous for doing the opposite, and it was not lost on me that both went to London schools. One was Angus Wilson, who went to Westminster, and the other, Kingsley Amis, who attended the City of London. Both their accounts report on a spirit on tolerance, though not, be it noted, of easy going. Standards were high; both schools count as Public Schools and are members of the Headmasters' Conference, but both are exceptional in this category for being for the most part day schools. Most of Westminster's boys, and all of the City of London's, are day boys. Where practically all the boys are young commuters it is clearly impossible to exercise the kind of regimentation usual in a boarding-school. Nowhere can be pronounced 'out of bounds'; there is no option but to trust the little bounders to find their way there and back by bus, underground and train, or a combination of these (in my day they included tram) and being also little Londoners we took this in our stride, whatever mischief we might get up to on the way.

Any boy is likely to approach his first 'big' school with a certain dread and I was no exception. On my first day I was acutely conscious of being among so many boys after years at what had almost been a girls' school, and books about 'Public Schools' had led me to expect rough treatment on principle. I saw these boys as sophisticated Londoners who knew a lot of things I didn't but I kept quiet about my ignorance and they with their London preoccupations, to my relief, didn't seem to notice. There was certainly no concerted ragging of new boys and it took me little more than a week to acclimatise and feel a little Londoner myself.

'The City of London School' was a proper name for it. Not only was it unique for being situated within the City, just inside Temple Bar, but most of the boys' fathers worked in the City, and its Board of Govenors was appointed by the Corporation of London. On Speech Day aldermen, in full regalia with the Lord Mayor at their head, graced the platform of the Great Hall, and the school's OTC annually supplied a contingent for the Lord Mayor's Show (I was once in it myself and very exhausting I found it). Its main endowment came from lands left by one John Carpenter who'd been Town Clerk of the City in 1442 but its official foundation had been in 1834 at the time of the first Reform Bill. It also had links with the Inner Temple, just across the road, and Temple Choristers attended it as of right, as well as a number from the Chapel Royal choir. In so far as it prided itself on musical activities it was thanks to them. The headmaster in 1920, Dr Arthur Chilton, D.D., was in fact not particularly musical – towards the end of my school career he once professed astonishment that anyone could sit at a keyboard and play 'all those notes' from memory – and on special occasions we had the Temple Choir to entertain us with madrigals and the like, under the leadership of Thalben Ball. 'Master E.A. Lough', who became nationally famous in the 1920s for an HMV recording of Mendelssohn's 'Hear my prayer' and 'O, for the wings of a dove', was one of them.

Dr Chilton, in appearance, was stern and a little terrifying; seemingly one of the 'old school' from whom the cane might have been expected but although he didn't rule out the cane, and was the only master allowed to use it, in fact he rarely did so and as the years passed I found him to be very just and understanding. He will also have had more say than anyone in the choice of masters and for this it would be hard to fault him. One master after another impressed by his personality, his learning and his capacity for putting it across. Perhaps 'the City' were able to pay good salaries but this won't have been the whole of the matter; all institutions are coloured by the personality of the man at the top. As for our fees, I once happened to see the bill which Father received for a term's tuition and noted that the basic fee, for one term, was 10 guineas (£10.50) plus cost of books, extras, etc. and even in those pre-inflationary days this wasn't a large sum.

The school assembled every morning at 9 o'c sharp. All the boys except the sixth-formers entered by a side-entrance in John Carpenter Street whose gate was firmly shut by one of the porters at zero-hour; anyone who was late had to come in by the august front entrance where his name was taken by the Head Porter and he would be on the mat. We assembled – 800 of us – in the Great Hall and having reduced ourselves to silence watched while the sixth-formers, with due decorum, mounted the platform and ranged themselves in an arc at the back, followed by the masters, followed by Dr Chilton looking his most authoritative. He proceeded to make announcements of general interest and then paused while a considerable number of boys trooped out. On my third morning I asked the boy next to me who they were, 'Jew boys', he whispered. The Jews trooped off to one of the larger classrooms where they had their own prayers while Chilton read Cranmer's 'General Confession' to us Gentiles. It was new to me but I heard it so often that before long I knew it by heart (and can recite it still). The school was officially non-denominational but no one seemed to fuss about that. After prayers we trooped out in an orderly manner and went to our several classrooms, becoming less and less orderly on the way.

From the very first day I noted smells. One was hair-oil. This was a thing it had never occurred to me to use but it was obvious, in the bright summer days of 1920, that some boys did so lavishly, thereby recalling an advertisement I'd seen of a bronze-coloured, oval tin box brimful of a green, semi-transparent semi-solid: "'Pears' Solid Brilliantine'." For a time, in my nostrils, it was the smell of 'London'. Another was of 'Lifebuoy' or 'Sunlight' or some other hygenic soap. During the lunch hour the boys played fives, or playground cricket with tennis balls, in the vast tarmacked playground and washing was necessary thereafter. At the bottom of each staircase were a few washbowls set in a slate slab with – usually very wet – towels hanging close by; often the scene of a good deal of splashing and mucking about, occasionally ducking. A further smell, at playground level, was cooking. Very few boys would have had time to go home to lunch so we had it laid on, at 1/3d a time (about 6 pence); one bought a book of twenty 'Dinner Tickets' for an initial outlay of 25/- a book. I shortly found I could save most of this money for my own purposes, go without lunch, stave off the worst pangs of hunger with a Whipped Cream Walnut, or Chocolate Turkish Delight (each costing 2d.) at the tuck shop and make up for the loss by a large meal when I got home.

Once school was over all London could be our playground and there were various attractions fairly close by. One supposed attraction was a newsagent just round the Blackfriars corner where copies of 'La Vie Parisienne' and 'Le Rire' were on display, with drawings of girls with huge tits and lecherous old men feeling them though it was more the daringness of such pictures than their lasciviousness which attracted; we were too young to be much affected. More interesting were Lyons' Tea-shops which were thick on the ground. There was one by Blackfriars Underground station and another at Ludgate Circus, both within a couple of hundred yards of the school. The latter was one of the first to introduce a soda fountain and had a curious sweet smell mixed with that of gas and tea-urns. Some of my lunch money was sometimes squandered on an ice-cream-sode or, in moments of special temptation, a

Knickerbocker Glory which cost the huge sum of a shilling but seemed worth it. It came in a long inverted glass cone and included strawberries in syrup covered with a strawberry ice covered by raspberries in syrup covered by a vanilla ice, the whole crowned with pistaccio nuts and a dollop of cream. It staved off the pangs of hunger better than anything. Yet another smell, which pervaded the whole neighbourhood, was of printer's ink and associated paint smells. We were next door to 'Fleet Street' and could catch glimpses in basements of strange machinery where bright vermilion ink was processed. A daily sight was of carts bearing huge rolls of paper on their way to the presses, each marked 'FIVE MILES OF NEWFOUNDLAND PAPER'.

A price that had to be paid for the school being in central London was that its sports fields had to be elsewhere, in our case in Catford, and later Grove Park. This meant that, except by boys who happened to live near them, they were used only on Wednesday afternoons and Saturdays. For most of us it also meant quite a lot of travel; in my own case a journey to Liverpool Street, an underground ride to St Paul's station, and a further train from there, plus the whole in reverse when coming home again, and I had to get the money for the Catford fare from Father. Miss Jones's regime, though comprehensive scholastically, hadn't extended to games and on my first few visits to Catford I found myself such a beginner that I decided to use the money for other purposes and spent my Saturday mornings exploring other parts of London. Rather to my surprise I escaped the attention of the few masters who encouraged sport though in fact these were not numerous in relation to the total staff; the school was unobtrusively free from sport fetishism.

Not that my Saturday morning explorations could really be regarded as more worthwhile activity. They chiefly consisted of wandering round the West End and looking at the glossy black-and-white photographs outside the various theatres. Enthusiasm for the theatre stemmed from Peter Pan; from then on it had had unquestioned magic, part of which was the proscenium arch with its huge curtain parting, or rising, to reveal scenes of wonder impossible elsewhere ('theatre in the round' would have seemed a great come-down). I did it so often that the years have become a little confused but a sort of composite memory includes Gladys Cooper at the Playhouse, José Collins at the Winter Garden, 'Fred and Adele Astair'at the Gaiety Theatre, 'Tea for two' and 'I want to be happy', and 'the Co-optimists' at the Prince of Wales Theatre in Coventry Street (a revue which reverberated as resoundingly at that time as 'Beyond the Fringe' forty years later).

On the Underground, at Mansion House station, large posters announced 'The Immortal Hour' by the Birmingham Repertory Company, and 'The Beggars' Opera' – 1500 performances! – at the Lyric Theatre, Hammersmith. Uncle John (Gerrard) had by that time bought a gramophone and one of his records was a 'medley' (typical of that philistine, pre-BBC period!) of tunes from the Beggar's Opera whose label revealed that they were played by 'the 18th Century Orchestra', which included a 'harpsichord' (then an unknown instrument to most people). I listened to it with the kind of entrancement that Vaughan Williams remarked on when he first heard certain folk-songs; tunes that one knew one had never heard before yet which one seemed to have known all one's life and which penetrated deep into childhood. A bit which particularly carried me away was in fact not traditional; it had been composed by the arranger, Frederick Austen; an entr'acte entitled 'Molly Brazen'. To me it spelt (still spells) 'the 18th century' and a London of which I'd had no idea until then but which in due course sorted itself out as part of London's past, especially when walking through the Inner Temple, as I did almost daily. The eighteenth century was being discovered by many thousands besides myself at that time, and one element in its attraction was nostalgia; a past which seemed wonderfully remote and more secure than the present. 'The Immortal Hour' evoked an even more remote, fairy-tale past – the Celtic Twilight – and its 'Faery Song' was for a while almost top of the pops.

Despite my interest, however, visits to the theatre were rare. My knowledge of London was confined to the daytime and its more central districts. I could see from maps on the Underground how to get to Hammersmith but I could also see that it was a long way and it was years before I actually went there. Buses, too, announced destinations whose names became familiar for this reason but I never went to the places (and am still unsure where some of them are; a boy in my class lived at Clapton but if I wanted to go there now I should have to consult a map to find out where it is). Museums were sometimes the object of my wanderings and I was appalled at the distance I had to walk to get to the London Museum to see a 'working' model of the Great Fire of London (of 1666). Much closer to the school was the British Museum which was considered interesting because of the naked statues in its basement but on the way there one passed Gamages and Bassett Lowkes in High Holborn and I was usually side-tracked into gazing Gauge 0 and Gauge 1 locomotives.

The boys in fact lived in widely scattered parts of the Great Wen and although I usually learnt from the ones I talked to where they lived, the names seldom meant much to me. We rarely saw one another away from school and there were only one or two occasions when I entered a schoolfellow's home, or he mine, and then only because we happened to live within cycling distance of each other. Another boy in my class commuted daily to Leigh-on-Sea, a journey of nearly 40 miles. Our homes, in fact, could be more than 50 miles apart and we often had no idea of the background to other boys' lives. There could be moments of 'truth' in the surprised discovery that the other was a Methodist/Evangelist, etc. I had such a moment in the Classical Third when a fellow I'd been sitting next to for some weeks, named Saint, one day revealed, by pulling a sort of necklace out of his pocket and asking 'Do you know what this is?' that he was Catholic. I was suprised but by that time I knew him as a human being so that it didn't seem to make much difference and I merely asked 'Is it a rosary?'. I couldn't see my way to treating him any differently because of the knowledge.

The same incuriosity applied to class. We were a mixed bag socially but I never heard anyone being taunted because of humble origin. On the sole occasion when there was a whiff of anti-Semitism it came – most exceptionally – from a master. His name was Gardener, the form-master of the Classical Second and house-master of Seeley. Our six Houses were purely nominal; a device for dividing us into competing teams for sports purposes since some sort of loyalty was needed as an impetus to win, and I'd been allocated to 'Mortimer'. The Houses were named after the school's founders or after Old Boys who'd become famous, and Mortimer had been almost the first headmaster and had set the school's tone.

Gardener had been a mountaineer, and an accident the previous year, which had occasioned a term's absence, had disfigured his skull and closed one eye. His ugly appearance, however, had probably little to do with his previously formed personality. (He was what would nowadays be dubbed 'a bit of a fascist' but this word, which was only just coming into use in Mussolini's Italy, was in no one's vocabulary at the time.) He was a British Imperialist and it can't have been an accident that his House commemorated the author of 'The Expansion of England' – as well as 'Ecce Homo'. He greatly favoured those of his class who were in Seeley with the corollary of looking down on those who weren't, and made no secret of it.

With a new intake in his form at the beginning of the Christmas term his first act was to go through all our names and attach them to our persons, and one boy gave his name as Hooper. We all knew him to be a Jew, as well as intelligent; an amiable fellow with a permanent grin on his face. Gardener, having noted his name, and probably wondering whether it had been changed from Goldschmidt or something of the sort, glared hard at him with his one eye and then said, in a tight-lipped manner: 'You've got an ugly grin on your face, Hooper. I propose to take it off by Christmas'. The unfortunate Hooper, who'd done nothing to deserve such a threat, stared down at his desk but involuntarily continued grinning whereupon Gardener, even more tight-lipped and in an even deadlier silence, repeated word for word what he'd just said. The word 'Jew' wasn't mentioned but we all sensed what was behind the remark. Far from making us anti-Semitic, however, it rather did the opposite; it was so manifestly unjust. In any case five-sixths of us were not in Seeley and so were under the shadow of disapproval ourselves but few of the much-favoured Seeleyites were impressed. It was quite out of keeping with the general tone of the school.

On another rather exceptional occasion class-consciousness reared its head and again it was a master who caused it, though probably unwittingly. He was a Frenchman named Laffitte who taught French to the entire Senior School. We called him Tootsies but had nothing against him; he was a good teacher and had sufficient sense of humour, as well as command of English, not to be vulnerable to ragging so that, by and large, we respected him. His unintended victim was a Scholarship Boy, a youth so grey and undistinguished that even his name escapes me. Whatever abilities enabled him to win the scholarship were not apparent to us. He was serious and studious, certainly, but a complete loner. (I should be interested to know what sort of contribution he'd have made to 'John Bull's Schooldays', given the opportunity.) We knew well enough that his background must be humble; he had a cockney accent and his clothes were poor but no one ever bothered to tease him. He was inconspicuous enough to be merely there and nothing more; without being aware of it we ignored him.

It was his clothing that caused the trouble. Tootsies one day addressed a question to him and then, while waiting for the answer, exclaimed: 'Why, you're not wearing a collar and tie!' In fact the boy had never done so; he wore an old grey shirt with no more than a visible collar-stud to close the neck-band (shirts in those days always had detachable collars; 'collar attached' came later) but it was only when Tootsies drew attention to the fact that most of us really became conscious of it. The boy, however, said absolutely nothing. He cast his eyes downwards and in the silence that had descended we noticed that a tear was trickling down his cheek. That was all. Tootsies switched his questioning to another boy and made no further mention of the matter. I did notice, however, that thereafter he wore a collar and tie.

No school can prevent a certain amount of bullying, especially one as large as ours, it happened independently of the rules. During my first year, when we were around the age of ten, there was a boy named Hodd who seemed about twice the size of the rest of us, an early developer with no great brain power. His main pleasure was to knock smaller boys about and we went in terror of him. We even ganged up on him. On one occasion when we saw him coming we hid in a sort of shed at the side of the playground to avoid him and got hold of a large beam of wood to hold against the door. He banged his massive carcase against it while we held on in panicky dread and then, when we'd almost given up, we were rescued by the bell. During the ensuing holidays we were rescued even more providentially; on the first morning of the next term we learnt from Chilton's announcements that he'd been killed in a road accident. The news occasioned no moaning at the bar as far as we were concerned.

There was another fellow who took pleasure in bullying, though more out of hate than because of his physical advantage. He picked his victims with discrimination and enjoyed seeing them cringe. One day he tackled a boy named Mumford who was capable of bullying smaller boys himself but who, on this occasion, allowed himself to be knocked down and have the bully's feet tread on him without making the slightest resistance. This was just the sort of triumph the bully enjoyed. Mumford's reaction was no doubt a good demonstration of 'turning the other cheek' but as I was one of the smaller boys whom he sometimes bullied my own reaction was to feel a certain contempt for both parties. One day it came to my turn but I found myself quite unable to follow Mumford's example; although normally a bit of a sissie and not the combative type I felt a surge of indignation, lost my temper and flailed the bully with blows in a way that was not particularly boxer-like but took him completely by surprise. It took me by surprise as well; I hadn't realised how much power and courage a lost temper could give one, and he let me alone thereafter.

I learnt a great deal from this encounter, chiefly formulated in the motto 'Be not afraid'. Easier said than done, very often, but I found it was the right approach and was helped in a curious way if one added 'Trust in God'. If someone was determined to have a fight then let it be clear that it was his doing but, given that, face up to it and if necessary take it on the chin whilst fighting back as doughtily as possible. Any hurts sustained in the course of doing so would soon wear off and in the meantime one's morale was higher. I found, however, that it was necessary to feel annoyed and the experience didn't make a boxer of me. A year or two later there was a 'boxing class' in the gymn and I found myself required to fight against a chap with whom I was quite friendly. It seemed to me silly; I had no quarrel with him and made a lamentable job of it. There were amused reactions to my inadequate performance, including some from the gymn-master, but there was no pressure on me to make myself more bellicose. It was not a compulsory class and I was excused boxing thereafter.

The personalities of the various masters were probably what had most influence on us in the long run but appreciation of them often came slowly. We were likely to have other preoccupations at the time. In my own case, no doubt by reaction to having been so much among girls and feeling myself a bit of a sissie, I tended to associate with some of the livelier, not to say wilder, boys; got into bad company in fact, to the neglect of my studies. After I'd been there a term or two I was one day reproached for this by Mr Troubridge, my first form-master ('Such a pity!') and felt the reproach the more when he died, very young, a year or so later.

For the first year or more we moved up a form a term and it wasn't until I got into the Classical First, in which I spent a year, that I really became conscious of its master's personality. He was an elderly Yorkshireman named Bertenshaw and in the course of a lifetime's teaching had acquired little tricks of speech which came out without thinking. One was 'I am so' ('have so', 'will so') added for emphasis. Criticizing some recalcitrant for an unpardonable mistake he would say 'I'm disgusted with you Sir' – he called us all 'Sir' – and then, when a slight titter from the class suggested that he was exaggerating, added 'I am so', to show he meant it. His most derogatory adjective was 'rubbishy'. 'Sir', he would say with appalling frankness to a boy whom he considered unworthy, 'You are a rubbishy person'.

He wore a small pointed white beard and once a month would have it trimmed, and his hair cut, during lunch hour. For some reason this always made him very bad-tempered and we soon learnt that it was a time to keep out of trouble. One day a boy, a Jew named Barnett and a shocking chatterbox, failed to observe this rule. He sat nearest the door which was one that blew open easily so that he often had the job of shutting it and one hair-cut day was unwise enough to fool about with it, shutting it and opening it with the pretence that it wouldn't stay shut until Bertie suddenly lost his temper, battered him about the head with a book he happened to have in his hand, picked up his satchel and threw it to the back of the room while books and sandwiches fell out of it. I can still see the look of wild agitation on Barnett's face as he rushed to the back of the room to rescue his property while the rest of us watched in awed silence. It was another demonstration of the power of a lost temper, and the more so since it was quite exceptional. For the most part Bertenshaw was quietly humorous and we learnt a lot from him. It was under him that we first broached Shakespeare – with *As You Like It*, the set play for that year, and far from being put off Shakespeare, as many seem to be at school, I learnt to appreciate him (and can still recite 'All the world's a stage' which we were required to memorise).

Moving up to the Classical Second meant having Gardener as form-master. The anecdote already reported about Hooper shows one aspect of him but is perhaps a little misleading as he was a perfectly good teacher in a hum-drum sort of way. One day, however, he made scathing references to 'the League of Nations'. This, I felt, entitled me to regard him with disapproval, even with a certain contempt. Having absorbed a great deal of propaganda on behalf of the League and heard my parents and others talking about it I reckoned I could understand the kind of thing that had led to the Great War, (then only four years behind us) and felt no doubt that we should make common cause with other nations against an aggressor but Gardener talked as if that war had never happened. Britain and the British Empire were unique and even European nations were lesser breeds. To doubt the Holiness – and apparently the permanence – of that Empire were to him akin to heresy and automatically made the doubter a cad of the lowest order. As I didn't want to give him an excuse for regarding me as one I kept quiet about my loyalties but I was in any case not a Seeleyite and so could hardly hope to stand high in his estimation. I knew I couldn't be one of his favourites. Fortunately I only had one term in his form and then passed on to the Classical Third.

This meant a man named Delavigne – pronounced Della-veen – one of those lucky schoolmasters, like Chilton, whose very appearance strikes awe into boys and whose manner backs it up. He looked, and could be, quite terrifying and although we slowly discovered him to be not only reasonable but occasionally humorous he was nevertheless a person with whom one didn't take liberties. As a result he had no problems of discipline and never gave punishments; we listened to him attentively. He would often emphasize important points by almost yelling the vital word or phrase, and I can still see him pointing to a chalk circle on the blackboard and saying: 'All these points LIE on the circumference' and hearing the word 'LIE' echo down the corridor to be overheard in other classrooms. He had no favourites, or if he did he never let it show.

Under him we did *Hamlet*, the set play for that year, and more soliloquies had to be learnt by heart including 'To be or not to be'. Memorising it I became aware that Hamlet/Shakespeare was not taking the Christian certitudes of death and resurrection entirely for granted:

> That undiscovered country from whose bourn
> No traveller returns, puzzles the will

And makes us rather bear those ills we have
Than fly to others that we know not of.

This seemed to be an admission of ignorance. I didn't yet know the word 'agnostic' but I'd heard of 'free thinking' and this suggestion that Shakespeare might have been a free-thinker, although not mentioned in class, marked a stage in my own capacity for it. I could quote him as an honourable antecedent.

Shakespeare was given particular attention during the Easter term which had no end-of-term exams; instead there was a declamation session devoted entirely to hearing these famous speeches, with prizes for the best declaimers. For once I was among them, in fact it was the only subject for which I ever won prizes. There was, however, another speech which made a deep impression on its own account; at the very start of the play Marcellus, one of the sentries, reassures his frightened fellows with:

Some say that ever 'gainst that season comes
Wherein our Saviour's birth is celebrated,
The bird of dawning singeth all night long,
And then, they say, no spirit can walk abroad;
The nights are wholesome; then no planets strike,
No fairy takes, nor witch hath power to charm,
So hallow'd and so gracious is the time.

As a child I'd once woken on Christmas night, acutely alert to its magic, wondering whether Father Christmas had yet made his visit, and then heard the cock crow. It was probably about 6 a.m. but it seemed to me like 'the middle of the night' and it enhanced the magic. To find Marcellus/Shakespeare reporting a similar experience seemed to touch a deeply personal nerve and put 'Shakespeare' in a different category. I'd docilely accepted him as 'great', part of the canon; I hadn't expected to have, as it were, a 'special relationship' with him.

(Although I still possess several of my school reports – and very depressing reading they make! – I regret I haven't Delavigne's. Misbehaviour was so unthinkable in his class that it ought to have been a better one than most. All the later ones tell the same tale: 'Has intelligence but no application'; 'Moderate; should be much higher'; 'Fair; would be much higher if he were less restless in class'; 'Very good or very bad; doesn't seem to mind which' and so on, all re-echoing Troubridge's 'Such a pity'. I've never really understood why I misbehaved my way through school to such an extent though I think I was more concerned with impressing the other boys – or certain other boys – rather than the masters. I liked to be thought daring, and if possible funny. It may have been camouflage to protect me from taunts of being a sissie; I'd discovered that one way of deflecting bullies was to make them laugh.)

In the earlier part of my school career there were other, more understandable distractions from study. Entering at the age of ten, or thereabouts, meant that within a year or two puberty, with all that that involved, started overtaking us, and as boys develop at varying ages its manifestations lasted over two or three years, especially for a late developer like me. I entered the school entirely ignorant of the 'facts of life' and the same evidently applied to most of my classmates as it was not long before intimations of them began to circulate. The fact that they were incorrect was not fully appreciated; we knew nothing of the orgasm; the man put his thing into the woman's and peed there and in due course a baby grew and had to be cut out, hence the navel. It didn't sound as though it could be quite correct but intuition suggested that there was some sort of truth behind it. It was certainly interesting enough to be passed on to Isabel, my confidante, three years younger but with short hair like a boy's. Isabel in turn passed on this interesting information to a little friend of hers, Jeannie Polly – short for Polychrondiardis; her father was Greek – and the Polly family were a great deal less prudish than ours. Jeannie went home and asked her mother if it could possibly be true. Mrs Polly, who was at that time having a baby herself, was indignant and complained to Aunt Elsie who passed on the complaint to Mother and I was on the mat.

As might be expected, Mama's handling of us was weakest and most inadequate in matters of sex. In addition to the usual Victorian inhibitions and taboos she'd had no brothers of her own age to enlighten her. Moreover she, and most of her generation including Papa, had been brought up on the maxim, where 'evil thoughts' were concerned: 'Put such thoughts out of your mind', 'Don't think about it', and had evidently been too obedient, or respectful of authority, not to comply. Not to think about it was virtuous and we were enjoined to do the same. Where Pen was concerned she may have had a certain success but I was a different matter. This was probably no surprise to Mother; boys were known to be difficult and she may well have been conscious of her ignorance of them and their wicked ways though I suspect she failed to address her mind fully to human sexuality and appreciate it was 'instituted of God', even if 'in the time of man's innocency'. Reflection on how she herself, her sisters, her parents, Mr Gladstone, Queen Victoria and the rest of the human race were engendered was a thought she will have put out of her mind and felt virtuous for doing so.

When she summoned me to the mat, therefore, and asked me, in a tone of appalling seriousness, what I'd been saying to Isabel I found it quite impossible to tell her. I remember saying 'I can't tell you because it's so awful', not doubting that it was 'wicked' and unsurprised when it was made a matter for Father to be told about and so for a thrashing, my crime being not so much talking about a matter which I wasn't supposed to think about as talking to Isabel in particular, leading the young astray, setting a bad example, etc. It was also no doubt felt necessary that Aunt Elsie and Mrs Polly should learn that justice had been done. Needless to say I was not told the true facts of life. These had to wait for a year or two by which time, thanks to learning about masturbation, I had a very sizeable idea of them but needed parental confirmation that I'd got it right. I knew it would be fairly useless, as well as embarrassing, to ask Mother but I could call Father's bluff by an appeal to the Holy Scriptures. Bible-reading was entirely permissible so I 'innocently' asked him one day what was meant when Amnon, in the Book of Samuel, said to Tamar 'Come, lie with me, my sister'.

Father probably suspected that I'd heard something so, plucking up his courage with a deep breath, said fairly bluntly 'Well, you know the real difference between a man and a woman, don't you'. If he'd kept up this blunt, man-to-man tone of voice and confined himself to physical details all would have been easier but of course morality and religion had to come into it and I was given to understand that, within wedlock, it was all rather sacred whereas without wedlock it was 'one of the most wicked things a man could do' (he probably had in mind *Tess of the D'Urbervilles' et al*). I was fully prepared to believe him but would still have liked to know why, and in more detail. Not thinking about it could be good advice when applied to something which you knew all too well but had to put up with, but applied to something you didn't know all about, and very much wanted to know more about, it was asking for trouble, a positive invitation to think all the harder and apply to others for information. I'd known almost since infancy that there was something 'special' . . . ('magical', numinous . . . the words came later) about 'private parts' and experience at Miss Newman's had shown that the same went for other children but the matter had come almost to the surface before that.

When I was about three years old, possibly less, and young enough to enjoy getting into my parents nice warm bed on a winter morning, I lay there happily staring at the ceiling with its 'damask' paper pattern, discovering that I could adjust my way of looking at it so that at one moment it seemed about a million miles away and the next so close as to be almost on top of me; (a sort of intuitive perception of the macro-/microcosmic; a feat I've been quite incapable of repeating since; 'trailing clouds of glory do we come'). Father, by this time, was having his cold bath and then Mother suddenly noticed that I was touching my genitals, quite innocently but it was enough to terrify her. In shocked, hushed but severe tones she said 'You must *never* touch yourself there!' thus alerting me to a taboo subject and arousing an intense interest where little had previously existed. By doing so she pushed me into a kind of double-think which lasted for several years. I could believe it might be 'wicked' but at the same time I could hardly fail to notice that when I entertained 'rude' thoughts 'it' got stiff without my touching it, and it followed as the night the day that whenever I saw an opportunity of finding out more from other children I leapt at the chance.

When puberty broke out among my schoolfellows, therefore, I was an alert pupil and boys seem to be more physically curious than girls, perhaps because they have something to get hold of – and to show. At puberty 'it' grows almost abruptly bigger, they feel proud of it and keen to show it off to those they can swank to. As a late developer I might have made my own discovery later than the others but I was also pink-faced, amenable (and I suspect rather pretty) boy and so a prime target for those ahead of me to demonstrate their new found pride and joy to. At quite an early stage in my school career I was taken 'across the playground' by a boy (whose name – as he has since been knighted and is well-known in the City – I suppose I had better suppress, though he was a charming fellow whom I recall with affection) and there, 'in the bogs', he pulled out what seemed to me a huge 'cock' and invited me to feel it. That was all. He made no attempt to demonstrate what might be done with it and I fancy he hadn't yet discovered himself; he was simply proud of it.

Intimations of what might be done with it first came from a Temple Chorister though I only knew about this at second-hand. It was in Bertenshaw's class that the contagion broke out like an epidemic and there was an interesting diversity of ways in which the knowledge manifested itself. Some boys were very secretive; one could tell that they knew, indeed could sometimes guess from their appearance – dark round the eyes – that they'd become addicts though they never talked about it. At the other extreme were a few who, when Bertie was out of the room, would fish out their cocks and get busy on them almost regardless of being seen to do so. The discovery of 'the feeling' had made them love the instrument which could provide such ecstacy.

We sat in pairs and even when Bertie was in the room there could be a good deal of furtive feeling in one another's pockets, often by invitation. My own induction arose out of this. The boy I was sitting next to (never mind his name) followed up such an invitation with a further one to accompany him across the playground when the class was over and there, in the bogs, he whanged away at it, meanwhile informing me, rather jerkily, that he 'did it six times last night'. I was too inexperienced to doubt it, being uncertain quite what 'it' was, unprepared for the climax and of course amazed to see a hitherto unknown substance pulsing out. When I got home I tried it out myself but it didn't work. I had to wait a couple of years before I could achieve the same miracle though 'wait' is not quite the word as I never ceased to attempt it.

Having once eaten of the tree of knowledge we mostly had an appetite for more, chiefly out of curiosity about other chaps' pricks, though some were shyer than others. Being so often a target for seduction I became less shy, even a little sophisticated, and bold enough to try out a little seduction in my turn, only to discover that some were not easily seduced, though there were other moments when I was astonished to find that So-and-So, a boy whom I'd never associated with sex, turned out to be just as interested, sometimes intensely so, even if more secretive about it. And there were some who, thanks presumably to a very strict upbringing, never took part in these activities. They included all the Jews. The Jews knew all about it – and told some of the filthiest jokes – but I never came across one who actually participated, (and am still curious to find out why not.) After all, plenty of us Gentiles had had strict upbringings and for all of us it was Forbidden Fruit. We all accepted that it was 'bad for you' and weakened you but we were less inhibited than they were. (Were they perhaps self-conscious about being circumcised?)

With hindsight I can see that the masters knew far more about what was going on than we gave them credit for. One master, named Cattermole, who took us for handwriting and geography, was notoriously bad at discipline and his classes were prime time for such misbehaviour but he never seemed to notice and I now suspect that he was perfectly well aware of it but, either to avoid embarrassment or because he thought it inevitable and didn't matter much anyway, never said a word to check it. Even Gardener, who might have been expected to disapprove for athletic reasons, must have preferred not to notice as it was in his class that one of the most flagrant acts of sailing near the wind took place.

This was the work of a boy whose name and initials I remember very clearly as we often sat next to each other, his name beginning with F and mine with G but although he is now dead I will forbear to mention it as I know he sent his sons to the school and as likely as not now has grandsons there. He was an early developer, as well as an ace gymnast, and the owner of a much-admired weapon. He sat in the front row! yet one day gave a demonstration for his immediate neighbour and the two of us in the desk behind. He took his time about it, with slow inconspicuous strokes, and when he reached crisis point removed his hand from it, drew his handkerchief out of his pocket, placed it in readiness and finally ejaculated into it while we in the desk behind craned out necks to watch this absorbing spectacle. How Gardener could fail to be aware of what was going on I don't know (in fact now feel sure he must have known). F, however, was one of Seeley's prize athletes and Gardener evidently decided to turn his blinded eye.

As we got older it ceased to be an interesting novelty and such behaviour in class a thing of the past but it remained a matter for discussion, usually on the theme: How long since you last tossed off? Pacts were made to see how long one could go without doing it, and it was a matter of strict honour to admit to it if you fell. The average was about three-and-a-half days. It you got as far as four you were doing well, and if you exceeded five you felt almost entitled to a free one for being so virtuous, even to two if the other chap had fallen in the meantime. If you both arrived at five and a week-end lay ahead it seemed common sense to agree on a free one for both parties. Sometimes one would report, in a determined voice, 'I've given it up' but we soon learnt to interpret this as meaning 'I did it last night (and wish I hadn't)'. Implicit in all this was obviously the assumption that it was better not to do it but also the recognition that not to do it at all was impossible. For several years after the initial discovery it was in nearly everyone's thoughts.

There were no love affairs, or not in the Junior School. Even in the Senior School there was no outlet for them since a day school has no dormitories. Any 'sleeping together', if it occurred, did so in private houses unbeknown to anyone else. No one was ever expelled, or if he was it was done very unobtrusively. F did in fact leave before he got as far as the Fifth Form, i.e. when he was rising sixteen, but we were given to understand that his father had a job lined up for him in the City and we had no reason to doubt it. (He was not the type to get himself knighted, however. I met him many years later and was struck by how much less of an athlete he appeared at the age of forty-five or so. He seemed rather a scruffy litte runt.)

Commuting back and forth between home and school inevitably laid us open to the attentions of 'dirty old men' and I had experience of this at an early age. A man – by no means old – got into my compartment at Chadwell Heath, when I was alone in it, and wasted no time in coming to sit beside me, stroking me on the knee, and asking me about life at school. 'I bet you get up to some good games, eh?' he said, but although I could guess what sort of games he had in mind it didn't occur to me to fend him off by talk. I cast a covert glance at the Emergency Chain but reckoned that if I attempted to pull it I should land myself in a struggle with him and come off worse. By the grace of God, however, the train wasn't held up outside Romford, for once, and as we were slowing down in the station he got out and disappeared, no doubt into another compartment. Although somewhat shaken by the experience I didn't mention it to my parents but I did report it to one or two cronies who used the same line.

I then found that they had a London sophistication about such things. They told me about a man known as 'Old Horny' who frequented some of the trains we caught. According to them he would get into a compartment full of boys, pull his cock out and invite them to feel it. He was clearly fairly harmless and the reaction of the boys seemed to be more amused than anything. I was told that one boy had accepted the invitation while the rest looked on with interest. I never ran into him myself but by that time felt half-disappointed; I, too, would have been interested, given the circumstances.

My sophistication increased when we moved to Surrey and used a line which served at least three race-courses: Epsom, Gatwick and Brighton. Members of the racing fraternity, it seemed, had a tendency to be interested in boys and for the most part their technique was much superior to that of the Chadwell Heath man. They didn't wait until there was no one else in the compartment; they'd manoeuvre one foot so as to touch your foot, even when there were others present, and I quickly learnt to read the signal and know what would be toward when the others got out. I also learnt that the best defence was talk – on some pretext or other. Get him into conversation and you could not only form a pretty good idea of the kind of man you were dealing with, you could deflect him into other channels. They could usually be got to talk about racing, a subject in which I could feign an interest and which invariably interested them. As a result I found all of them harmless, sometimes even quite amusing. It was another application of the 'Be not afraid' principle and I never found it unsuccessful. There was even one occasion when I felt confident enough to allow some intimacy, though it went no further than an examination of each other's parts. I was curious to know what a grown-up cock would look like and was rather pleased when he said of mine 'There's many a girl would be glad of that'. I suppose this was sophistication with a vengeance but I can't really say I regret it; it seems to me preferable to ignorance and I find it hard to see that any harm was done thereby.

A Rise in the World

Father's move to Surrey marked a major watershed in my life, and I was the more conscious of it because about a year elapsed between knowing we were going to move and actually moving. Not only was it a change from town to country, with an entirely different set of people to know, but it was shortly succeeded by puberty so that it was almost a change from childhood to young manhood. I call it 'Father's move' as I knew he'd one in mind ever since the war but it would have been no surprise to learn that it had been Mother's idea in the first place. I became aware that she'd found Romford pretty limited; with its farmers and Congregational church-goers it had always seemed to her more 'Jim's' place than hers. In a new home among new neighbours she could feel herself on a more equal footing. Moreover it was going to be a larger, detached house in half-an-acre of land, and what housewife wouldn't be pleased at such a rise in the world? – especially one who'd had a long period of comparative penury as a young women.

We knew about it a year in advance because the site was bought before the house was built on it. The post-war development which had been going on on all sides in Essex was going on in Surrey too, and the new site was in a village no one had ever heard of: South Nutfield. Father had heard about it from 'a man at the office' and, having once committed himself, went there nearly every week-end, partly to see how the building was getting on but chiefly to start work on the garden which had to be made from scratch from what had previously been rough field. For his summer holiday that year he took a tent and he and I camped out there so as to work on it the more intensively while watching the house grow. On one occasion he gave the bricklayers half-a-crown 'to buy yourselves some beer', a fact which I found the more striking as he didn't much approve of drink. In such a good cause, however, it was clearly wise to keep the men in good heart and half-a-crown (two-and-a-half shillings) would have bought them several pints of beer. They later thanked him saying 'We drank yer very good 'ealth, Sir' and I was conscious of a different accent from that of Romford; the r's were slightly burred and gave their speech a more countrified air.

The house, like the garden, was also being architect-designed from scratch and in that period of New Departures and a World Free from War both Mother and Father were determined to make a good thing of it. Father bought a book called 'The House we Ought to Live in', by John Gloag, and for a year or two it became their bible. Details culled from it now bring vividly alive again that house that became 'home' for thirty-five years:

> 'The house we ought to live in will . . . mean a house where work is simplified, cleaning reduced, and convenience increased . . . Generations of architects and furnishers have ignored the daily duties of the housewife, and in the planning of their work have upheld the respected adage 'cleanliness is next to godliness' with exemplary thoroughness by providing as much material as possible to keep clean.
>
> Every working apparatus in a kitchen should be so placed that it can be used easily and without effort by anybody. Accessibility and convenience do not end with the kitchen; they affect the position of door-knobs and staircase handrails, the arrangement of window frames so that the view is unimpeded, the height of the lavatory basins, the design of cupboards, and so forth . . .
>
> Draining boards should be fitted in each side of the sink with plate racks above . . . Below the shelf of the serving hatch there can be drawers for cutlery.

A combination of china-cupboard and hatch with double-doors fitted immediately above and below the hatch level could be planned to cut off the kitchen atmosphere more successfully.

Should a scullery adjoin the kitchen it must have the same floor level . . . The presence of a step and a lower floor level makes for danger, discomfort and general inconvenience.

Inside the porch a large mat sunk to the level of the floor is desirable. The bathroom has a heated towel-rail.'

The first and most striking contrast with Romford was the matter of soil, and we knew the land before the house was there to be known. South Nutfield is in the Surrey Weald, just south of the Greensand Ridge, and the soil is a solid, sandy clay. One needed a special spade, locally known as a graft, to dig it; a long straight spade with a curved blade and a sharp edge. One dug into this soil like so much cheese – when it was soft enough; when it was baked hard in high summer digging was out of the question. Given a soft enough condition one cut quite narrow slices of the stuff; a large clod of it was not only abominably heavy but would in any case need slicing into smaller pieces, and getting weeds out of it was an arduous and unsatisfying business. When one got below the topsoil it was almost pure yellow – in prehistoric times it had been river silt, I learnt – and its solidity could have its advantages. When we later came to dig a lily pool we found we could cut a neat pit with perpendicular sides which stayed that way until the cementing was done.

I say 'we' as if I did as much as Father but it was he who slaved away at it, his pride and joy, and devoted nearly all his spare time to it for many years. His ambition included a tennis-lawn though the digging and levelling of this was a job he had to get done professionally. To have a tennis-lawn in one's garden wasn't everyone's luck and it made me a differently oriented person; I'd moved into the 'Freda Barrington' class. In succeeding years my chief contribution was to keep the lawns mown, and the tennis-lawn was not the only one; by the time he'd knocked everything into shape there were two others, as well as grass paths and numerous grass verges, all of them my responsibility though they also became my pride and joy. With all the grass cut and the edges trimmed – a couple of hours' work – the place looked so nice that I felt proud of it too. I also became familiar with the names of plants and shrubs and thought nothing of using such names as Galega Officionalis Alba, or Lobelia Cardinalis – but I am jumping ahead.

The house was finished early in December and to avoid taking too many days off from the office, Father arranged for the move to take place over the Christmas holiday. Two days before Christmas we went to Croydon, spent the night at the Aunts' and on Christmas Eve, 1923, got up early, took the South-Eastern – by that time almost Southern – train through Purley, Coulsdon and Merstham, changed at Redhill to a train for the Tonbridge line and finally disembarked at 'Nutfield'. Father explained that the village of Nutfield was really a mile to the north and South Nutfield had grown up much more recently around the station. The house was so newly completed that it hadn't dried out and we had to light fires in all the rooms, including the four bedrooms. By the time the removal men arrived it was snowing gently, seemingly Surrey's baptism of the familiar pieces of furniture as Copsey's men from Romford carried them into their new, quite different setting, but with this new winter countryside around me which I could now regard as 'mine', and the sense of the past which Christmas brings, I was inevitably reminded of Marcellus' speech that we'd just been studying and felt the time to be 'hallowed and gracious'. A new life was beginning and the omens seemed propitious.

At the time it was built the house was on the fringe of the village and the view from our rear windows was of fields and a gently rising hillside with elm trees in the hedges dividing the fields. (By now it is within hearing distance, almost seeing distance, of the M23.) It was fairly unspoilt countryside and I brought to it notions picked up from reading. I hadn't yet learnt to appreciate the ambience of the stockbroker belt, indeed hadn't yet learnt this expression, and didn't immediately realise that the wealthier inhabitants of the neighbourhood, some of them very wealthy indeed, were all City Gents, and most of the villagers their servants, gardeners etc. A few genuine farms still survived though most of them were 'home' farms of the wealthy, but for me it was George Eliot and Jane Austen country and I saw the village children as potential playmates. I was very hurt when I found them jeering and rather hostile.

There was one respect in which it might still be regarded as Jane Austen country and that was in the matter of social 'calling' carried out by ladies. When newcomers moved into a neighbourhood its inhabitants, via the bush telegraph, would take careful stock of them and decide whether their status, both social and financial, warranted recognition of their existence. Most of the scrutiny and assessment was done by the wives but they usually had to get their husbands to check on the newcomers' financial background in the City – or elsewhere – and the two jointly had remarkably sensitive antennae as to whether they'd be gaining or losing caste by calling at the newcomers' house, chatting briefly, and leaving their cards. Even when it was decided that a call was warranted it was still possible to indicate limited approval by making the call a very brief one – and of course adopting a lofty and patronising manner – and something approaching disapproval could be conveyed by calling at an outrageously early hour after lunch, thus embarrassing the housewife who'd barely had time to change into her afternoon dress, and leaving again almost immediately. The normal call spread itself round 'afternoon tea' during which there would be social chit-chat while the two ladies took closer stock of one another. When she left, the calling lady would leave her 'visiting cards' on the silver tray on the hall table, i.e. small slips of what was called 'pasteboard' with the names engraved thereon in copperplate. For some reason the wife's cards were larger than her husband's and two of them were left as against his one. This implied social recognition and the newcoming lady was expected to return the call shortly afterwards.

Jane Austen made it clear that the bush telegraph was both speedy and well-informed in her day but by 1923 things were much facilitated by an organisation she would have known nothing of and which would have caused her much suprise, viz. the Women's Institute, founded during the war with the declared aim of getting country people of all classes in touch with one another and 'improving the conditions of rural life'. In the early days the Chairwoman was usually the Lady of the Manor but at least there was some social contact between the classes. Mother was introduced to this at an early stage – an operation which didn't involve formal calling – and mutual scrutiny was therefore possible before anyone took the plunge of calling. Class consciousness was acute and with it went money-consciousness. Some of our wealthy neighbours had come up in the world and one in particular was a 'war profiteer'. It was a far more snobbish place than Romford and although Mother was not greatly worried by it our status was in face enhanced locally when it became known, as it did with remarkable speed, that Pen's fiancé came from a moneyed family.

My own chief reaction to all this was to become accent-conscious. I'd already noted peculiarities of the local speech, such as pronouncing 'how' more as 'ho', but at the other extreme there were some altogether-too-posh vowel sounds from some of the 'Stockbroker's wives'. It had the effect of making me check my own speech for possible inadequacies, a process begun by the Aunts to counter the influence of Sunday School. Taking my cue from Father I was impatient with snobbery but I didn't want to give the snobs any excuse for looking down on me. I did, however, go through a phase of feeling inferior for attending a mere day school when most of the stockbrokers' sons went to schools like Haileybury, or at least Tonbridge.

It went without saying that I was railway-conscious. I now lived on what was rapidly becoming 'the Southern' and had twice as long a journey to London daily. Since the Amalgamation my season-ticket was valid for the ex-LBSC as well and I could sometimes get a non-stop from London Bridge to

Redhill and have the pleasure of tearing through East Croydon and seeing that footpath from the train instead of the other way round. Much more exciting, however, was an express which ran through Nutfield daily, half of whose carriages were Great Western. Research revealed that this was another sort of Sunny South Express which served the Channel ports and south coast at one end, thence via Redhill, Guildford, Reading, Oxford and Birmingham to Shrewsbury and Birkenhead – for Liverpool – at the other. My enthusiasm for railways, far from diminishing, had increased, and much of my schoolboy reading fed the appetite with technical and other information. Wandering round London on Saturday mornings I'd always included the main termini; on a well-organised day I could see off the Flying Scotsman from Kings Cross at 10 a.m. followed by the Cornish Rivera Express from Paddington at 10.30, making a careful note of the names of all locomotives in the process, meanwhile feeding myself on half-pound slabs of chocolate. Paddington's Platform 1 was closely associated with Nestle's Walnut Milk; Kings Cross, for some reason, with Cadbury's Milk, Fruit & Nut. Brazil Nut Milk was another possibility but it was more expensive and so eaten less often, and if I was hard up I contented myself with Cadbury's Milk which was only tenpence.

Paddington Station impressed by its spaciousness, as well as the different look of the engines; they didn't have 'domes', they had brass safety valves, and their rather squat funnels had copper rims; they looked sleek and powerful. The cream and chocolate livery of the carriages was also rather exciting and nearly all of them announced their destinations on long plaques along the top: PADDINGTON, BRISTOL and WESTON-SUPER-MARE, etc. The spaciousness was due to the fact that Brunel, the founding father of the GWR, had reckoned on having the wide gauge until obliged to give in to the majority, but it suggested a reason why the GWR might be considered – and certainly considered itself – the aristocrat of railway companies. Brunel had also been concerned to keep curves and gradients to a minimum and his main line to Swindon allowed some of the fastest running the country (still does). A further device I'd read about was a water-trough between the rails from which the engines could renew their supply whilst running at speed. Engines were constantly in need of water and the hydrant with its elephant trunk was a feature of nearly every station, too familiar to be noticed most of the time. All this interest made me the more conscious that the Great Western was the only major line I'd never travelled on and I was accordingly most excited when it turned out that some of our visitors to the new house lived on it.

One was a cousin of Father's who was always known as 'Cousin Alice' and 'Trowbridge' was mentioned several times in her conversations with the family. When I first heard it I exclaimed: 'Isn't that on the Great Western?' and she replied, 'Yes, Bryson, the only line that hasn't changed its name'. This was a new thought. I'd read the placards which listed the old railways now comprised in the new groupings, and the Great Western had its own small share of additions at the fringes, mostly in Wales, but in fact it had been singularly unaffected by them and for the most part went on its old, majestic, leisurely way, not obliged to adjust its methods and habits to those of others, still less alter its name to suit them.

Another visitor was an old school friend of Father's whom we'd rarely seen but the new house was clearly something for him to come and admire and by a curious coincidence he too lived in Trowbridge. He came with his wife and a son of my age for the week-end and the net result was a counter-invitation for me to spend a week with them during the Easter holidays, 1924. When the time came Father gave me my ticket – bought at a railway office in the City – and told me to get into the 'Westbury slip' at the back of the train.

The train was the 1.30 to Penzance, second only in importance to the Cornish Riviera Express which covered the same route and, thanks to water troughs, was non-stop to Plymouth. The 'Westbury slip' meant the last two carriages and the ticket collector stressed the importance of this. They were labelled PADDINGTON, WESTBURY, FROME, YEOVIL and WEYMOUTH and I got into the very last compartment, which was empty. The door, I noticed, didn't spring shut with a 'slam' lock as did those of suburban trains; the solid brass handle had to be turned by hand to its closed position and did so with a weighty click. Everything about the train seemed weighty and solid.

Once it had started, negotiated the many points outside Paddington and got onto an uninterrupted stretch of line it seemed to have a different 'hoofbeat' from others hitherto. The sound of iron wheels on an iron track was an inescapable part of any railway journey (and how quickly the feather-bed springing of nowadays has made us forget it!). Every time a wheel crossed the tiny gap between one rail and the next there was an audible click and since most carriages had a bogey of four wheels at each end, this meant a constant clickety-click, clickety-click. Without looking out of the window one could tell how fast one was going by the speed and frequency of those hoof-beats. One could also tell when one was approaching a station by interruptions to the regularity, due to negotiating points. 'A train going over the points' at high speed through a large junction could produce a wonderful cannonade of clicks.

Whether the GWR's hoofbeat was really different I couldn't be sure but by then it prided itself on having 70-foot carriages which must have affected the spacing of the beats and my hyper-sensitive antennae might well have picked up the difference but I also had other preoccupations and having a compartment to myself meant that I could rush from one window to the other and poke my head out. Thanks to Brunel and the absence of curves it was not often I caught sight of the engine – the train was in any case a very long one – but I noticed with interest the water-troughs between the rails of the up-tracks. (On a later journey, when I was in the front carriage I once put my head out to see the engine picking up water and got my head soaked with the spray of it.) As we were slowing down for what turned out to be Reading I saw vast beds of flowers and a notice reading 'Sutton's Seeds' and shortly afterwards Huntly & Palmer's biscuit factory. I didn't notice Reading Gaol, not then having heard of it.

The 1.30, unlike the Cornish Riviera, stopped at Reading – only 40 minutes after leaving Paddington! – and I had time to notice the immense width of the platforms – again this spaciousness! – after which we sped through Reading West, Theale, Aldermaston, Midgham, Thatcham – although we were travelling 'at speed' it was still possible to read the names of the stations –, all new, unknown fascinating places. I felt myself in strange new country (and still associate 'Aldermaston' with river meadows and meandering streams lined with willows and kingcups). Further on we sped through a station called 'Savernake Low Level' – 'Change for the Marlborough Line' – and alongside a canal which went through a tunnel. Beyond that, on a distant brown hillside, was a White Horse. I'd read about this in Tom Brown's Schooldays but hadn't appreciated how its prehistoric, almost sinister presence seemed to dominate the vast valley over which it looked.

At Paddington, what with the length of the train, the fact that I was in the last carriage and the practice of attaching the engine only a few moments before departure, I hadn't risked going to see what was hauling us – it would certainly be a King or a Castle – but reckoned I'd do so when we reached Westbury. I'd reckoned without the Westbury slip, however. When we finally slowed down and came to a halt in Westbury station there was no engine and hardly any train; we'd been slipped off and the rest of the train was by then well on its way to Frome. This explained why my end compartment was so very abruptly an end without even a guard's compartment to back it; the guard's compartment was at the front of the other carriage and it was his job, just outside Westbury, to pull a level and detach us from the rest of the train, let us slow down through simple loss of momentum and finally bring us to a halt in Westbury station. There were similar slips at Taunton and Exeter so that the non-stop section which finally drew up at Plymouth would be a very much shorter train. Quite an ingenious device but chiefly of advantage to those travelling from London; people in Westbury, Taunton and Exeter who wanted to get to Plymouth would be less amused. Moreover it wasn't feasible in the opposite direction; you could hardly have a couple of carriages catching up with a moving express and latching on to it so the 'up' Cornish Riviera stopped at all three stations. I should be able to catch it going home.

In the meantime here were Mrs Godbold and Brian on the platform to meet me and lead the way to another, more humble but still interesting train at another platform, on the way pointing out another White Horse on the hillside above. It looked more of an old Dobbin than the one above Marlborough but it was nevertheless impressive. I was clearly in another, quite different country.

Trowbridge was permeated with the hoppy smell of Usher's brewery, and had several old inns which made Romford's – and Redhill's – seem industrial by comparison. It was also, I discovered, in 'Dairyland'; there was a centre where large milk 'churns' were delivered and wheeled expertly about – as they were at the railway station by porters. And the bells of the parish church played a hymn tune on the hour. A 'provincial town' with its own architecture, its own preoccupations and so its own savour, which made me aware of a much older agricultural England. Together with its surrounding Wiltshire and Somerset it broadened my horizons by providing living illustrations of things I'd read about or studied at school The first White Horse had been one such, and from the train windows I'd noticed fields which seemed to be 'ribbed' with low symmetrical undulations and suddenly realised that these must be the remains of the mediaeval 'strip' cultivation of which we'd been told. Mr Godbold ran a draper-and-carpet shop and specialised in making his wares available to country folk who had little opportunity to visit the town. He was exceptional in owning a tiny Austin-Seven in which he drove about the district taking orders and sometimes delivering them, and Brian and I were allowed to accompany him so that I was introduced to villages 'far from the madding crowd' – a quotation I already knew. Book-learning was beginning to marry up with direct experience, while the latter accumulated in readiness for further education. He would visit farms in remote areas where the farmer's wife would invite us in for a cup of tea in front of the kitchen fire and exchange local gossip with him in her Wiltshire brogue. Sometimes he would stop at an inn for lunch in villages of unimaginable quietness and eat pickles and cheese while chatting to the landlord. I wasn't given, and didn't expect, a glass of ale but to go into a bar at all was a new experience; and all this was enhanced by the fact that it was springtime; primroses and 'lady-smock all silver white' not only made me Shakespeare-conscious but embalmed the whole experience in a kind of magic.

Cousin Alice was a schoolmistress who lived with her father, a former professor of Mathematics at Lucknow University who died a couple of years later. She was a great admirer of the eighteenth century and nearby Bath had some prize examples of its architecture to show. The district was also rich in reminders of the early Industrial Revolution. The Kennet-&-Avon Canal that I'd seen from the train was one manifestation of it and there were many other canals in the area. At Devizes, with Mr Godbold, I'd seen a whole 'staircase' of canals. Some of them – so notices proclaimed – were the property of Great Western Railway who, I learnt, had bought them up to eliminate their competition. She also pointed out early weavers' cottages with long horizontal windows for giving good daylight to the handlooms within. All this fitted into what we were learning at school about the Industrial Revolution and I could visualise how the children of the cottages would be required to help with the work.

Cousin Alice, who was a well-read cultivated woman, had a way of making everything seem interesting and Bath, under her tutelage, was an education in itself. Not only its eighteenth-century architecture but the Dickensian Pump-room – though its water tasted horrible – the Roman baths and, not least, the beautiful fifteenth-century Abbey. I'd learnt from the Children's Encyclopaedia about 'Gothic' architecture but I'd never seen fan-vaulting before and I was entranced by it; 'Perpendicular' was added to my list. On the way back we stopped at Bradford-on-Avon and visited the Saxon church, only recently uncovered, and a new category dating from before the Norman conquest was further added. What with the Decorated church at Lacock and the Early English of Salisbury cathedral, church architecture got fairly thorough treatment.

Yet another outing was to Great Chalfield Manor, a mediaeval manor house which, she said, had been virtually independent, producing its own food and wine, growing and weaving its own woollen cloth and forging its own implements. The juxtaposition of these visits and seeing one period grow out of another made me increasingly history-conscious though it was a lesson which had happened unawares in the holidays. Nearly all these outings were by train (some of them on lines which no longer exist).

Although undoubtedly 'a lady' Cousin Alice was interestingly different from the Aunts. Like them she was of Scottish descent and, again like them, had had no brothers (or sisters for that matter) yet compared with them she seemed wordly wise though in fact she'd led the most sequestered of lives. For several years she'd been a schoolmistress at Ogbourne St George (even now one of the quieter places under the sun) but no doubt a school would give her insights that the Aunts lacked; she'd find out about boys and their wicked ways there but she was far less censorious than they or my parents. She knew how to handle children and although I saw less of her when very young I doubt whether it would have occurred to me to be naughty in her house. That she could entertain critical thoughts about people without feeling it necessary to express them was revealed a year or two later when Mother, Father and I were staying there. I had a bickering match with Father which, for us at that time, was all too normal but in her house I suddenly became conscious that it was not normal and remarked, by way of apology, 'The trouble with our family is that we're all too fond of keeping each other in order', whereupon Cousin Alice half-pleased, half-embarrassed me by exclaiming 'Hear, hear!'.

She also impressed me with her ability to play the piano. As a nicely brought up Victorian girl she'd naturally had piano lessons but she played much better than most. Her party pieces were usually Chopin waltzes and at family Christmas gatherings she used to enchant us with these, and me still more with Schubert's 'Moment Musical' in F minor. In her little semi-detached house she had many valuable items of antique furniture and I was particularly impressed with an oak court cupboard with the date 1641 carved on it. She told me it had formerly been in Bongate Hall, Appleby, where she'd lived as a girl, in Westmoreland, (and my most cherished heirloom; because I admired she left it specifically to me). After this initial visit 'Cousin Alice' became a treasured institution for Isabel and Sandy as well as for me; a person one could easly go and visit in 'the west of England'.

Caught in this web of recollections of those early South Nutfield days is a memory so different that it seems only by chance that I recall it, I suppose because it had no future, though it had a vivid present. Isabel and Sandy, almost brother and sister to us since we had identical grandparents, in fact had an older sister, Tricia, so far unmentioned. Tricia tended to be left out of account because she was mongoloid (what is now called Downs Syndrome), a grievous misfortune for parents which can in due course become one for brothers and sisters, but as children we were quite unworried. We took it for granted that Tricia sucked her tongue and had a bad circulation so that if you pressed a finger on her purplish flesh the spot remained white for a long time. We knew she couldn't play hide-and-seek properly but we happily let her play along with us and made allowances. She was an accepted part of the scene and it was regarded as a great joke when, on her eleventh birthday, she went round saying 'I'm a lemon'.

Isabel and Sandy had been frequent visitors to our new house but Tricia only came once, as a birthday treat. Thereafter she longed for a second visit but shortly afterwards we learnt that she was ill, then, from Uncle John on the telephone in a very concerned voice, 'Not at all well', then that she had rheumatic fever and then, like a bolt from the blue, that she was *dead*! It was a far greater shock than Grannie's death, or Aunt Catherine's; it was altogether too near 'home' and I shed sentimental tears thinking of 'poor little Tricia'. I also had the honour of representing the family at her funeral and for the second time in my life looked on death. It was a much prettier sight than Grannie's corpse had been. Death had largely removed her moronic appearance and her flesh, instead of being purplish, was pure cream. It was easy to see how Dickens might have described her as looking like a little angel and the feeling was enhanced by the smallness of the coffin.

Tears were of course shed at her funeral but I was too inexperienced to appreciate that there was less distress than there would have been for a normal child. Our childish sorrow was genuine enough but we recovered with remarkable speed and once home after the funeral Isabel, aged ten, was most anxious to exploit my presence in Romford and play demon patience. By then, aged thirteen, I was old enough to doubt the propriety of playing cards on such a day but a rather silent and moist-eyed Aunt Elsie made no objection when Isabel asked her permission so we played. When in due course I reported all this back in South Nutfield Mother's comments made me realise that it had in fact been a 'merciful release'; God, it appeared, had been Good again. A year or two later Uncle John bought a house in Purley and 'Tricia' became emblamed in an increasingly remote 'Romford' past but the memory of her, though rarely reflected on, is still ineffaceably there. In the past the death of the young was all too distressingly familiar but to come close to it, when one is young oneself, is to acquire a certain wisdom which those without the experience lack.

Crime without Punishment

When I was too young almost to remember it I once bit Pen's arm at the culmination of a quarrel and was 'punished' by being shown the toothmarks on her skin (I'm glad to say they drew no blood) but what I chiefly remember is the horror I occasioned and the shame I was made to feel. Some years later, sitting at the tea table, I was playing with an iron magnet I'd been given when the constant noise of it tumbling on the mahogany surface suddenly made Mother seize it and fling it into the corner of the room. For her, this was such an exceptionally violent act that I gave an astonished laugh and she herself was obliged to smile but it did the trick more effectively than a slap would have done.

Both my parents were good at giving reasons why a particular act or activity was not allowed but there could be the ocassional 'Do as you're told!' which provoked the suspicion that the real crime was Disobedience. They also made a point of being consistent; it was no use punishing an offence one day and overlooking it the next. It was, however, taken for granted that children must be punished when naughty; the two things went together and had the unspoken corollary that harm would result if naughtiness went unpunished. The punishments themselves ranged from 'no cake – or jam – for tea' to the stick or the strap or – the ultimate sanction – a thrashing from Father, with his bare hand on my bare bum, and it was the august solemnity of this which constituted a large part of the terror though in fact it was not a deterrent. We accepted the cliche that the punishment should fit the crime and rarely went on to ask ourselves what good would come of it but this solemn Act of Justice meted out by Father when he came home from the office and was told about the crime by Mother never seemed to me a very good fit. A serious, thought-provoking 'talking to' was always more effective, while a thrashing allowed me to feel that, the misdeed having been expiated, I could go back to square one. One or two crimes which received no punishment at all were what had the most profound effect in the long run.

One such occurred on that memorable Boxing Day when I went in the Gibson's newly-acquired car to Southend-on-Sea. As previously mentioned, 'word was sent round to our house' asking whether I'd like to accompany them but I omitted to mention that at the moment when that word was delivered – to Mother at the front door – I was in the back yard doing a war dance round Sandy with a carving knife in my hand. What was I doing with a carving knife? I think I'd been sent to clean it; in the days before stainless steel one way of polishing a blade was to push it up and down in the earth. Sandy, aged two, had wandered round from next door while I was doing this and it was his presence which prompted the dance. I circled round him brandishing the knife but was disappointed to get no reaction from him. Perhaps he was scared but it was characteristic of him to suppress all sign of it and stand with his back to me in sullen silence. I felt this to be a challenge and so got closer and closer to him until – unintentionally, but I'd been sailing too near the wind and knew it – I gave him a tiny stab in the back of the neck.

At first he seemed to take no notice but then, suddenly – and again this was typical – burst into noisy tears. At that moment Mother emerged from the back door to give me the Gibson's message and at once asked 'What have you been doing?'. Getting no reply she looked at Sandy's neck where a tiny slit was marked with a slight ooze of blood. I was well aware that I deserved . . . I didn't know what awful punishment for this crime but Mother disconcerted me by shedding tears and all I got were her horrified reproaches. They were almost enhanced by her telling me of the Gibsons' message and saying 'Well, you'd better go, and get out of the house where you can't do such things!' or words to that effect.

They were certainly much more emotional words than I was used to hearing from her and I fancy it was this, and the unaccustomed tears, which did the trick. She was genuinely worried at what a little devil I sometimes seemed to be and this had the effect of making me worried myself.

Certainly having Isabel and Sandy to show off to contributed a great deal to my naughtiness, indeed younger playfellows generally were an immediate incitement to misdeeds which wouldn't have happened otherwise. Not that my crimes were committed solely in their company. I mentioned earlier stealing small sums from a supposedly secret drawer where the collection money was kept, in order to go to the cinema, and these thefts were never discovered. I was fully aware that I was doing wrong but if the desire for something was strong enough it swiftly acted as the mother of invention. For a while I had a mania for ice-cream and rapidly found a means of 'affording' one. Mother once sent me to get a smoked haddock from Thompson's, the fishmongers, giving me a gold sovereign for the purpose. The fish was tenpence and Miss Thompson looked at the sovereign disapprovingly. "Aven't you got anything smaller?' she asked. The fact that I hadn't meant that she pretty well cleaned out the till in order to give me change, of which at least two shillings had to be in 'coppers', and 24 old pence weighed about a pound, quite apart from heavy florins and half-crowns. Thompson's, however, was next to Baldwin's, a sweet shop – the smell of smoked fish, of which serried ranks of smoked haddock, kippers and bloaters hung about the shop, was inextricably blended with that of sweets in my nostrils – and having cast lustful eyes on the goodies in Baldwin's window as I came past it didn't take much mental ingenuity to work out that I could lighten the weight in my pocket to the extent of a penny by buying a penny cornet – which would be finished and out of sight by the time I got home – and then tell Mother that the fish had cost elevenpence, which seemed a likely price.

Having got away with it I continued the practice whenever I was sent shopping and nearly got caught by becoming reckless. One day I had quite a shopping list and added a penny or two to nearly everything that hadn't a known price, failing to notice that one object had the price marked underneath it. Mother therefore challenged it and although I managed to lie my way out of the difficulty somehow, it was a nasty moment and made me more careful in future. I sensed that she might not believe me and this had disturbing implications. In the past punishment had followed crime as a matter of course and to be suspected of a crime meant to be accused of it. Not to be thus accused, although clearly under suspicion, was somewhat disconcerting; what was Mother's real opinion of me?

At school Justice was in many ways less magisterial than at home. Chilton believed in sparing the rod while taking care that the child was not spoiled, and correction mostly consisted in stern words pronounced ad hoc by the masters. The ultimate sanction was to be reported to 'the Headmaster' but I never heard of anyone being caned. The commonest formal punishment was 'an hour's detention' but for all my misbehaviour I only recall being given it once. It meant staying behind after school and doing some required task in the Detention Class, a class whose more positive purpose was 'Extra French' or 'Spanish', optional classes for a few boys who sat in the front rows while the detainees performed their tasks in silence at the back. It seems typical of the Crime-Punishment syndrome that I quite forget what I was being punished for while still remembering the first words of Spanish I ever heard – *'la flema castellana'* – through over-hearing Tootsies' lesson.

A crime I do remember was comitted in the Lower Fourth where, as a late developer, I was still at an age which most of my classmates had outgrown, and continued with outbreaks of fooling which at moments made Sprague, its form-master, furious with me. On one occasion I hurled a hard ball of paper at a chap on the other side of the room when Sprague was writing something on the blackboard but he turned round too soon, saw the missile, asked 'Who threw that?' and at the end of the class I was on the mat. He then reminded me of my various misdeeds and ended by saying, rather savagely, *'That's* what you want!' indicating by a gesture a sharp stroke of the cane. He was evidently reluctant to report me to Chilton, however, and finally let me go with a serious warning.

There was also an occasion when Laffitte got exasperated with me and ordered me to stand at the back of the classroom and learn by heart a paragraph from our current French reading-book: Prosper Merimée's 'Colomba'; if I didn't know it perfectly at the end of the class he'd report me to the Head. I took no chances, memorised it as if my life depended on it and at the end of the class recited it to him word perfect and in my best French accent (as a result of which I can still remember the last sentence: *Tout à coup la cloche du village tinta lentement, car un homme était mort dans la nuit*) but the mere fact of doing this served to emphasize the idiocy of my behaviour, as Tootsies didn't fail to point out.

When we moved to South Nutfield another mania led to my most disgraceful – and last – crime, viz.: model railways. The new house had a large loft and inspired by other fellows at school I slowly got together a Gauge 0 system. One of them introduced me to the Leeds Model Co. in Euston Road where scale models, lengths of line, 'chairs', goods trucks, carriages, signals and everything else could be bought in 'do-it-yourself' kits and put together at home, the money being found, piecemeal, from pocket money, lunch money, and presents. When Christmas or my birthday was approaching I let it be known that I'd like presents of money for this purpose and I used it with the utmost economy. Stations could be made up from cardboard and the like. Locomotives, however, were another matter; you needed to be a skilled engineer with your own workshop to make one of those yourself so I had to put up with an old clockword tank engine dating from years previously. Then one fine day Bassett Lowke advertised a 2-6-0 Mogul steam locomotive available in the liveries of the four railway groupings, at the price of 5 guineas (£5.25). One filled the boiler with water, lit a little spirit stove which fitted underneath it and when the water boiled, pulled a little lever and the thing tore off at a scale speed of about 120 miles an hour, whistling while it did so. After school the said friend and

I went and admired one in Bassett Lowke's window in High Holborn, indeed I lusted after it and thought of little else.

It was then that the devil – or was it perhaps my guardian angel? – set a snare for me. For some most exceptional reason both Father and Mother were away for several days which meant that I was fed by the maid but otherwise had the house to myself. Then a letter arrived from Father which stated 'I have mislaid a £5 note' and asked me to look in a wallet in his drawer and see how many fivers there were in it. If there were three, all was well; if only two would I please search the waste-paper-baskets to see if he'd accidentally thrown away the third. I looked and there were three but it seemed too good an opportunity to miss. I replied saying there were only two and that I'd searched everywhere but could find no trace of a third. That gave me £5. The remaining five shillings could be raised by selling my stamp collection which I accordingly took to Stanley Gibbons in the Strand, thereafter wasting no time in repairing to Bassett Lowke. Five pounds was a lot of money (it would be something like offering a note for £100 now) and I knew that at some shops one was required to write one's name and address on the back but I'd already decided on a fake name and address if Bassett Lowke did so. Much to my relief they didn't and I sailed home with my treasure under my arm and hid it in the loft where no one was likely to find it.

So far so good, but it could only be a matter of time before the family found out. In any case what was the good of possessing the thing if I couldn't show it off? I therefore concocted a story to account for my possession: a school friend had been given it by a rich uncle but as he had no railway to run it on and in any case had other interests he'd decided he'd rather have the money and I'd beaten him down to a pound, which I'd raised by selling my stamp collection. All very plausible, I thought. So much so that I almost believed it myself and when some time had elapsed and the engine had become a little shop-soiled I decided to anticipate the telling of the story by bringing the engine downstairs one day and showing it off as if I'd just acquired it, thinking that this would be more convincing than letting Father find out by chance.

What I didn't know was that Father had made a note of the numbers of his £5 notes and had asked his bank to find out where and by whom the missing note had been paid in. In due course the answer had come back: Bassett Lowke, High Holborn, and I was on the mat in the biggest possible way.

I'd become such an accomplished little liar that I repeated my story while still looking him straight in the eyes. He was naturally not at all inclined to believe it and I remember saying 'I can see it must look very fishy' but I nevertheless stuck to it and he said 'Well, I think you'd better invite this friend of yours down so that he can confirm it'. I said, 'Yes, I'll gladly do that' privately wondering whether I could persuade any of my schoolfellows to come and perjure himself simply to get me off the hook, but fortunately he didn't insist. I think he was torn between not believing me and not wanting to believe that his son could be such a little crook so he decided to let the matter go with what could clearly be seen as a warning. No doubt he also wondered what he could have done in the way of punishment if I'd pleaded or been proved, guilty. I was getting too big for thrashings.

In the event it worked though I don't really understand why. As with wetting the bed, I stopped abruptly and thereafter thieving, cheating and lying became virtually unthinkable. All my life since then I've tended to be almost pedantically honest and regarded anything to do with 'crime' with horror yet when I ask myself what effected this transformation I wonder whether the operative words may have been 'his son'. I think I must have felt that I couldn't live with such an image of myself, nor with him in such duplicity and he, come the crunch, was more important than railway engines. A serious 'talking to' had certainly been more effective than a thrashing would have been.

I am also struck, in 1983, by my reluctance to record all this. It has taken a painful effort to get it down on paper and much of me would have preferred not to do so. Many years after the event I debated whether to tell Father the truth but refrained because I couldn't see that any good would come of it. If I now rather wish I had it is partly out of curiosity to know whether he had any doubt of my guilt but decided to leave an open verdict in the hope that my conscience would do the rest, and partly because I could have reassured him that it did. Whether he could have cast any light on why it should have worked I rather doubt. As his own father had died when he was a mere ten years old he had no equivalent experience from his own past to guide him – though I find it hard to imagine him ever doing anything so dishonest.

An even more belated thought is: did Father himself set the snare?

A Classical Education

Although, on the Classical Side, the main studies were Greek and Latin, with due attention to Hellenic History and Geography, the curriculum included Mathematics, English and French, while one period a week was devoted to Science and another to Scripture. Mention of the subjects, however, at once brings to mind the men who taught them and I find it hard to say which had the more lasting effect.

Sprague, who'd inherited the nickname 'Gaius' – an indication of the extent to which he was identified with Latin –, has already been mentioned as the form-master of the Lower Fourth. Under him we pounded through Greek and Latin grammar and tried to get our brains round the Gerund and the Gerundive, or the difference between the negatives ου and μη. In the course of a long teaching life he'd developed one or two time-saving devices. One concerned the 'iota subscript' under a final omega; it didn't affect the pronunciation but one had to know it was there and Sprague's device was to make one hold up one finger to show that one knew. Similarly to indicate the 'nu-ephelkustikon' at the end of a word one held up two fingers (as for the later Churchilian victory sign). It was under Sprague that we had to learn by heart the Irregular verbs: *vinco, vincere, vici, victum et al*, and for hearing these he stood us round the walls of the classroom to facilitate rapid changes of place. If your didn't know the answer *instanter*, or if it was wrong, then it was 'Next boy', 'Next', and not a second wasted. Now and again he would pop in a question of his own as a matter of general knowledge, and there could sometimes be a long series of 'Next's' with a consequent spectacular move-up for the boy who knew the right answer. I remember once going from the very bottom to the very top by this means though I forget what gem of knowledge got me there. On one occasion he asked what was the expression used by gladiators when they paraded in front of the emperor before the slaughter and this produced a long line of 'Next's' before one boy (named Illingworth, ha!) came out with '*Morituri te salutant*' and Sprague peered at him before he moved up saying 'Yes, you know a thing or two, don't you'. It wasn't the first time that Illingworth – he was the boy who lived at Leigh-on-Sea – had revealed knowledge beyond the usual.

That I remember such details must mean that I learnt something from them, and it was not only *Morituri te salutant* but also Sprague's 'You know a thing or two' which I somehow recognised as a set phrase. On another occasion he introduced us to the very expression 'a set phrase', then new to me. I once even earned the accolade 'You know a thing or two' and although I've forgotten what it was I knew I can see that it may have been among the reasons why he refrained from reporting me to Chilton. I was clearly an infuriating boy in many ways, though I suppose not in others as I never felt myself disliked; I simply didn't take things seriously enough – or not the right things. (An inspection of Kennedy's Latin Primer, which we used in the Lower Fourth, reveals that where there was room on the blank pages, or even in the margins, there are pictures of railway points drawn in painstaking detail.)

Learning by heart was as important as it had been at Miss Jones's. There was no rhyme or reason about Latin and Greek Irregular Verbs, any more than there was about Avoirdupois Weight or the order of the alphabet; they simply had to be embedded where they could remain until needed (turning out, along with genders, to be useful mnemonics for the Romance languages). Homework, over and over again, was not only written work but memorisation. Gaius didn't disdain the use of an old piece of 'doggerel' – another word I first learnt from him – as a time-honoured *aide mémoire* for recalling the prepositions which took the Ablative:

A, ab, absque, coram, de

Palam, clam, cum, ex, and *e,*
Sine, tenus, pro and *prae.*
Add: *super, subter, sub* and *in*
When State, not Motion, 'tis they mean.

He also took us for English and despite inattention in class I managed to absorb a great deal of it. Our poetry book for that year contained chunks of Don Juan and Childe Harold, Shelley's 'The Cloud', 'Ozymandias' and the 'Ode to the West Wind', Campbell's 'Hohenlinden', and Southey's 'Battle of Blenheim'. Their period chimed in with the History we studied that year: the Corn Laws, the Speenhamland Act, the Reform Bill, etc.; a fat book entirely without illustrations. I found it boring whereas a great deal of the poetry stayed in my memory. (A few years ago, in a company of friends, somebody quoted 'There was a sound of merriment by night' and I found that to their amazement, and to some extent my own, I could complete the whole stanza and most of the following one. Gaius, thou should'st have been living at that hour!)

Mathematics was the province of a man named Hill, officially form-master of the Classical Fifth but an expert who taught Maths and nothing but Maths to the entire Senior School. He was a very tall, rather thin man with a muscular torso – his hobby was mountaineering – and a small pointed black beard, as well as a somewhat mischievous smile. It was recognised in the curriculum that mathematical ability was in a different category from other abilities; some who were brilliant at it could be pretty dim at other subjects, and vice versa. As a result 'Maths' was the occasion of a general post when each of us migrated to his 'Maths Set', quite a different crowd of fellows many of whom one didn't even know, some much senior, others much junior, and with Modern and Science Sides mixed up with Classical. I was weak at Maths but perforce worked my way up until one day I found myself in Hill's class and there, to my astonishment, I not only found it interesting but sometimes even managed to ask intelligent questions simply because Hill's own questions forced them to the surface.

One day, when the subject was dimensions and Hill had drawn a square on the blackboard and then, with the help of dotted lines, delineated a cube, I asked why it wasn't possible to illustrate the fourth dimension. Not really a very intelligent question but it showed the right kind of curiosity and Hill didn't disdain it though I didn't really understand his reply. He mentioned a seemingly impossible concept: space/time – Einstein and his Theory of Relativity were in the news at the time – on the face of it a three-dimensional object on the move. On another occasion he drew the top of a chessboard on the blackboard meanwhile telling us that, according to legend, the emperor of China, anxious to reward the inventor of chess in a suitable manner, had offered him anything he wanted. The inventor (it seems a beautifully Chinese, 'Kai Lung' sort of story!) modestly said that all he wanted was one grain of rice for the first square, two for the second, four for the third, twice that for the fourth, and so on 'and when they worked it out they found they hadn't got enough rice in the kingdom'. To begin with we were as incredulous as the emperor but Hill got us to work out an approximation of the number of grains of rice that would go into a cubic inch and went on to demonstrate what an almost inconceivable number is represented by 2^{63}. What chiefly stuck in my mind, however, was the way he fitted his patter to the chalking, half-turning to us from time to time with his imperturbable half-smile and stretching out a long arm to chalk up further figures while getting the multi-dimensional message across.

He drilled us so thoroughly in the techniques of solving problems using arithmetic, algebra or geometry interchangeably that, although almost a mathematical philistine, I not only got through Schools Certificate in Maths but actually got a *credit* in it! I also ceased to be afraid of it and had glimpses of the kind of vision it could offer. With another master I might well have written it off as a subject quite beyond me. (I find myself feeling the same sort of gratitude that I feel for Miss Jones. It would be nice to think that in those inconceivable dimensions that embrace us, something still identifiable as 'Hill' might get this message.)

Hill, who was probably an agnostic, was also Vice-Principal and on the rare occasions when Chilton was ill, or otherwise unavailable, he took prayers in the morning *ex officio*. Our vast Great Hall was notoriously difficult acoustically and although Chilton knew from long experience how to make himself heard, others less experienced could be wonderfully inaudible. Hill, however, seemed to have no difficulty at all; his resonant voice penetrated to the back of the hall without his giving the slightest impression that he was speaking loudly. Cranmer's General Confession sounded a different prayer coming from him.

Scripture – or Divinity, as he preferred to call it – was one of the few classes taken by Chilton himself. It was chiefly a study of the New Testament in the original Greek which, even without the advantage of knowing by heart a good deal of the King James version, proved very much easier than Aeschylus or Sophocles. Chilton also took us for Latin and Greek Verses. We spent one period a week trying to turn, say, a heroic couplet into a laboured artefact which added up literally, to a hexameter-cum-pentameter. It was like doing a jig-saw puzzle in which one exercised one's ingenuity by adjusting the size of the pieces; it seemed to have little to do with 'poetry' as I understood it. Latin poetry seemed to me in any case singularly artificial. I could appreciate the onomatopoeia of a line like '*Quadrupedante putrem sonitu quatit ungula campum*' in which the stressed syllables imitate the hoofbeat of a galloping horse but I was disgusted by their indifference to word order. The words were poked in wherever they could be made to fit by letter count – officially known as prosody – regardless of the aptness or otherwise of their juxtaposition: 'Four-footed (the) soft (with the) sound shakes (the) hoof (the) field' with both the adjectives divorced from the nouns they qualified. Chilton, however, proved much less formidable as a teacher than I'd expected. He treated senior boys almost as equals and seemed to regard this verse-making as a rather enjoyable piece of self-indulgence which we too could enjoy.

'Science' meant trooping upstairs to the top floor, a welcome break from hum-drum bookwork. It was reckoned that it would do both Modern and Classical scholars no harm to have at least an inkling of Inorganic Chemistry and one period a week was set aside for this. Up there masters by the names of Adlam, Rudkins, and Penn inducted us into the mysteries of such things as the electrolysis of water, thus making them a little less mysterious. It was the use of apparatus or, in the lecture room, watching the masters use it, which made these classes exceptional. It was a change to be doing something with one's hands or to witness visible signs of something happening. Inevitably it was only a smattering of the subject but it gave one an insight into what it was all about; made it an understandable subject, in fact, even when one was ignorant of the details. One of Adlam's demonstrations involved a 'catalytic agent': 'a substance which, while remaining unaffected by the experiment, by its presence allows the metamorphosis to take place' and it was Adlam's laconic, unimpassioned spiel while fitting out the experiment which stuck in my mind, while making the word 'catalyst' meaningful thereafter – and 'Science' a little less dialectically materialistic.

While we were being given this insight into 'Science' the Science boys were being given an insight into Latin though I never learnt from any of them how far that subject became meaningful for them. The senior ones would have Ellingham to teach them and he was not a master whose classes could ever be boring.

Ellingham was technically form-master of the Upper Fourth but as Hill was solely concerned with Mathematics he taught both Classics and English to the Fifth as well so that for two successive years we saw more of him than of any other master. He was a remarkable man whom it was impossible not to respect and, being comparatively new to teaching, he hadn't settled into habits in the way that old hands like Bertenshaw and Sprague had. He was of a younger generation whose remarks often seemed wonderfully sophisticated by comparison; on one occasion, getting us to list some tricky grammatical points, he suggested heading it 'Deathtraps for duds', a title which wouldn't have occurred to Sprague. He never gave punishments; it was sufficient to feel that one hadn't earned his approval. Trying to describe him to somebody, on one occasion, I said he had 'personality' and it was typical of the kind of stimulation he gave us that I should have cast around for what was for me a new word. At Oxford he'd been a Craven Scholar but although his main subjects were therefore Latin and Greek it was above all in English that, for me among many others, he opened up new horizons.

That I greatly admired him brought out other undesirable traits in me which must have exasperated him, though he was good at hiding it. I tried to shine, more or less, but above all to be noticed, to attract his special attention to my odious little self though he was not at all the type to show favouritism. He gave credit where it was deserved but to all alike and he refrained from high praise for anyone. For our English homework during the week-end he would require us to write verses, or an essay, or some other piece of composition and then, when he'd had time to go through them all, would devote a period to reading bits of them out to the class as illustrations of what was good or bad, but in doing so he mentioned no names. One might hear a bit of one's own handiwork read out with comments but even if these were favourable no one else would know that you were the author. Having done this, and given us the most useful insights in the course of it, he would hand back our various efforts with more searching comments written in red ink which hadn't been read out. In the margin of one rather purple passage of mine on one occasion was 'Don't rant'. On another occasion another purple passage had been used by him as an illustration to the class of a style inappropriate to the theme, 'too biblical', but he'd nevertheless given me nine-out-of-ten for it as a piece of good writing in itself.

Where Latin was concerned, much time was spent in the Upper Fourth on Cicero whose word order, although in prose, seemed to me almost as artificial as in poetry. The practice of putting the main verb at the end of the sentence, however far removed by subordinate clauses, could make the construing of a long paragraph something of a nightmare, especially if one had skimped one's homework as I too often had, and Cicero had some prize examples of the Accusative-with-Infinitive, and *ut*-with-the-Subjunctive constructions with the operative verb miles away down the page. When we did Pliny and Apuleius we found them very much easier but they were rather looked down on; Cicero was 'a much greater stylist'. All of them were turned to good account by Ellingham insisting on our translating them not into technically correct English but into properly turned English prose, thus teaching us as much about English as about Latin.

On a much later occasion he once spent a large part of one period getting us collectively to think up English hexameter-pentameters which would pass the Latin prosody test, writing up our suggestions on the blackboard as we went along to see whether they would do, and a still retrievable detail is the end of the hexameter line: '... wielded a —— crowbar'; a suitable adjective which was also a dactyl or a spondee was needed for 'crowbar' and I suggested 'ponderous'. By the sound of it a good suggestion and Ellingham wrote it in but only to demonstrate that its last syllable, having two vowels, however lightly pronounced in English, wouldn't pass the letter-count test; in Latin it had to count as a stressed syllable. The final solution, suggested by a chap named Hawker (how these details stick!) was 'silvery'. Not a very appropriate adjective but it passed the letter-count test. This might have been regarded as poaching on Chilton's Latin verse class but whereas with Chilton the end-result had been a piece of faked-up Latin Ellingham chiefly revealed to us the nature of English –and for that matter Germanic – poetry which was governed by the weight of words when spoken and for the most part took them in their natural spoken order. English verse which had been inspired by classical models might sometimes seem artificial by the standards of the present day – he instanced Gray's 'rosy-bosomed hours' – but even Gray was unlikely to divorce 'rosy-bosomed' from 'hours'. Ellingham wasn't a great admirer of Gray, however, and once shocked me by saying that he 'wouldn't give a thankyou' for the famous Elegy.

This contrasting of various languages, which extended to French, as well as the use of our own language in 'English' homework, with exercises in consciously different styles, were really the essence of our 'good education'. We were made into more articulate human beings with an increased capacity for seeing things with detachment, including ourselves as language-speakers, and the further it went the more we were obliged to consider appropriate vocabulary and so to think more clearly. An exercise set by Ellingham on one occasion was to write a letter of thanks to an aunt for a present one didn't want, e.g. a book which one already possessed, without being in any way insincere or hypocritical. In due course we had a period when extracts from our various letters were read out and one chap – anonymous of course – had written: '... and when I opened the parcel, what a suprise I got!' This struck most of us as brilliant; it was an eye-opener into ways of being evasive without actually lying.

'Rhetoric' was mentioned occasionally when we did Cicero and Demosthenes but Ellingham saw to it that the spoken word also received some exercise and thought up a device for making us use our brains fast, as well as our voices, and giving us practice in public-speaking, viz. the mini-debate. Debating subjects were thought up by us and put into a hat with our names in another hat. The first name drawn had to speak impromptu to the first subject drawn for two minutes, and the second name drawn had to oppose it for a further two minutes. The first name was then allowed one minute to reply and then a vote was taken. In this way we could get through about half-a-dozen subjects in one period. Thinking up a worthwhile subject wasn't easy but on one occasion, knowing that he was interested in music, I thought up 'That music should be part of the school curriculum'. I still suspect him of a bit of fiddling as the next thing I knew was my name being called. I was so startled that I didn't immediately rise to my feet and had to be commanded to do so, whereupon he gazed at his watch to observe the passage of two minutes. So startled in fact that I couldn't think of anything to say. I hadn't given much thought to the arguments in favour and so had no initial phrases on the tip of my tongue. I tried wildly to marshal a few thoughts but they got blocked at the exit, so to speak, and the more the awful silence solidified around me the more impassable the exit became, with the result that I spent the whole of the two minutes standing there speechless. He was quite merciless about it and said nothing to encourage me; he merely gazed at his watch and at the end of the two minutes called upon Harris, the next name drawn, to speak against the motion – not a very easy task as nothing had been said in its favour. I suppose I must have exploited my final minute for replying – Harris had given me something to go on – but such a minor detail pales into oblivion beside the almost traumatic experience of making such a fool of myself in public. It was nevertheless very salutary; I started thinking up arguments in favour of music being part of a school's curriculum from that point onwards – and expressing them in the most eloquent terms. Playing in an orchestra, or singing in a choir, simultaneously involves both individual expertise and very precise team work, and with results which, with any luck, will give pleasure to others. (Whether the incident induced Ellingham to marshall arguments in his own mind I can't say but not long after I left the school – and Chilton retired? – he did in fact start up a school orchestra and I believe it has had increasing success ever since.)

Eloquence could also be cultivated via Shakespeare. The set play was *Macbeth* which we studied so thoroughly that I could recite by heart the whole of the first Act and large tracts of later Acts, quite apart from the set soliloquies for which I again got the prize, (I'm relieved to be able to say). It must be rarely that a whole class of schoolboys is carried away by Shakespeare but thanks to Ellingham's enthusiasm we undoubtedly were. A further lift was given by the fact that, being lucky Londoners, we could take time off one Wednesday afternoon to attend a matinee and see Sybil Thorndike and Lewis Casson performing in the leading roles. We were completely bowled over by it, above all by the sleep-walking scene. Another scene which ran it a close second was the one in Macduff's castle when the Murderers kill his son. In class we'd savoured the boy's line: 'Thou liest, thou shag-haired villain!' and the Murderer's reply: 'What, you egg!' but we hadn't been prepared for the fearful screech the boy gave at the point of death and our blood ran deliciously cold. At the end of the scene we felt we'd been vastly entertained (though it's the kind of scene I can hardly bear to sit through now).

I doubt if Ellingham was a great theatre-goer, and this performance may have carried him away almost as much as it did us unsophisticated schoolboys but as a new master on the look-out for good teaching ideas he took the opportunity to exploit our enthusiasm and got us to enact bits of the play in class, bringing a few of us in turn to the front of the class where we had to perform it with as much histrionic ability as we were capable of. Most of us hadn't much but with the Thorndike/Casson performance hot in our minds we overcame our shyness and excelled ourselves. As a result I found myself standing in front of the class as Lady Macbeth (I was invariably cast for the female parts) and declaiming:

> Come to my woman's breasts
> And take my milk for gall, you murdering ministers
> Wherever in your sightless substances
> You wait on nature's mischief.

and since Sybil Thorndike had clasped her own breasts as she said this I did the same while imitating to the last syllable her declamatory tones. It was a measure both of Ellingham and of the effect the play had had on us that there was not a titter from anyone.

There were other lines in the play which we found eminently quotable, one being 'What bloody man is that?' which had managed to get past the censor. Our edition had been edited by Arthur Quiller-Couch and his – (or his publisher's?) – maidenly notions of what was seemly did not confine themselves to bawdry, of which *Macbeth* contains little. At the end of the play, when a white-faced servant comes to tell Macbeth that ten thousand soldiers have appeared against him, 'Q's' edition had made him say 'My curse upon the light, thou cream-faced loon'. This was too much for Ellingham who got us to restore the original: 'The devil damn thee black, thou cream-faced loon.' Editors were further exposed when, on the last day of term – a day when by time-honoured convention we could talk and generally misbehave – Ellingham persuaded us that the time would be far better spent if we used it to read right through *The Tempest* and asked everyone who could get hold of a copy to bring it with him. As a result about ten differing editions were being read from with a consequent losing of place and exclamations that such and such a bit 'isn't in my copy'. It was a revealing exposé of the kind of mischief editors had got up to, chiefly in the name of keeping 'the blush of shame from the cheek of modesty'. (Do they still, I wonder? How would a master in our Permissive society handle *Romeo and Juliet* with such lines as 'The bawdy hand of the dial is even now upon the prick of noon'? And I wonder how Ellingham would have handled it. I slowly discovered him to be surprisingly straight-laced in matters of sex.)

In one year, with Ellingham, we studied Spenser and in another Cobbett as part of the English syllabus but the emphasis was by no means solely on the writers of the past. We devoted much attention independently to 'Poems of Today' (Second Series) and 'Today' was 1922 (our card-backed edition, I now see, was a 1925 re-issue – and contains no marginal drawings of railway points). It included such old-stagers as Yeats, Belloc, Masefield and Newbolt, all of whom were still alive, but the majority were younger and less well-known. My own discoveries included T.E. Brown, James Stephens, Ralph Hodgson, and Seamus O'Sullivan, that is to say I found poems by them particularly memorable – and remember much of them still – but the discovering was really done for us by Ellingham. He didn't require us to learn them by heart; he sometimes got one of us to read them but my chief recollection is of him doing so himself in his own inimitable way. He didn't 'recite' them; his unimpassioned speaking of them could hardly have been further from the incantatory declamation used by Yeats – as heard on the wireless – yet we listened in attentive silence. His very lack of showiness was part of the fascination, though he would use dialect when the poem required it, e.g.

William Dewy, Tranter Reuben, Farmer Ledlow late at
plough,
Robert's kin, and John's and Ned's,
And the Squire, and Lady Susan, lie in Mellstock
churchyard now.

This was a poem of Hardy's called 'Friends Beyond', a poem whose 'pessimism' ran much against the grain of my youthful optimism but which nevertheless bit so deep that I remembered it whole.

I remember it still. It came back to me the night my own Father had become a Friend Beyond and moved me to tears. Years later still, I attended, rather exceptionally, an Old Boys' Day at Grove Park, sat at lunch with a very much older Ellingham and in the course of it found myself quoting what seemed an apposite comment on the occasion:

We've no wish to hear the tidings
how the people's fortunes shift;
What your daily doings are; Who are
wedded, born, divided; if your hearts
beat slow or swift.

He was delighted and by now I feel thankful he *was* living at that hour. It is all too rarely that one gets – and seizes – an opportunity to thank schoolmasters for stimulation received but one can see that for them it must be rewarding. He himself went Beyond a year or two later. I only just managed it in time. His opinions and even some of his casual observations remained criteria for me for a large part of my life and if, in the course of it, I came to see him a little more this side idolatry, the fact that it took me a lifetime to do so is a measure of influence he had.

Camp

There was of course a school OTC and although it was permissible for parents to maintain conscientious objection to their sons joining it, such objection was not encouraged, nor was Papa, with his Boys' Brigade background, prepared to be of their number. Twice a week, therefore, I had to go up to London in khaki uniform and, at the end of school, draw a Lee Enfield rifle from the armoury and go through with 'square bashing' in the playground. It did me no harm, in fact when Hitler's war overtook us the knowhow, in the matter of Slope Arms, Order Arms and the like, stood me in good stead but at the time, with my head full of anti-war propaganda, I was determined not to distinguish myself at it and almost made a point of failing Certificate A. The annual OTC camp at Tidworth, however, was another matter. In spite of myself I rather enjoyed it, but it was above all an eye-opener to the Public Schools of the kingdom and the types of boy who attended them; most of them very much more posh and some of them blatantly sophisticated. I remember staring incredulously at a youth in the NAAFI who was smoking a Turkish cigarette with a long holder and generally acting the tart. One of my schoolfriends described him as a 'proper nancy-boy' and it seemed an apt description. Although we were the Big City boys we were quite unacquainted with such decadence.

One night we had 'Night Ops', which meant being divided into sides and attacking, or defending, a 'position' somewhere on Salisbury Plain, and we were given a password to use if challenged. Failure to give the right one meant that one would be 'taken prisoner'. Fortunately I had no special responsibility;

I simply obeyed orders though the blundering about in the dark made little sense, nor did the ocassional Verey Light illuminate much beyond our immediate selves. It seemed clear only that the 1914–18 war was being re-enacted in mime. Several different sets of Night Operations were going on in other parts of 'the field' and at one point the patrol group to which I belonged stumbled into two fellows who were challenged by our corporal, a keen soldier named Pethybridge. They gave a password we hadn't heard before so Pethybridge said 'I'm terribly sorry but I'm afraid we'll have to take you prisoner', to which they replied, in very posh accents, 'O, for God's sake do! We're bored stiff with the whole business'. Much later, after a good deal of confusion, it was found that their password was for quite a different set of Night Ops. They'd wandered off into the dark deliberately, determined not to be interested. I never learnt what school they came from but I was evidently not the only one to feel anti-militarist though I was less courageously demonstrative about it.

There were various strict rules, one of which was that there must be no smoking after Lights Out, but on the last night it seemed that Authority turned a blind eye to this; there was a great deal of smoking and wandering about in other schools' 'lines'. There was also quite a lot of sexual misbehaviour and if I'd had more experience of boarding schools I should have realised that at one point I was being propositioned, rather diffidently, by a boy from Radley. Not that there were no goings-on among the CLS boys; there was a startingly and seemingly spontaneous outburst on all sides, as a result, presumably, of a week's hard training in such a closed community. Fellows who'd never previously shown much interest suddenly found themsevles entering into the general spirit of orgy which overtook us. 'Sleeping together' was a new experience for most of us. Meanwhile the masters/officers kept their distance, evidently regarding it as only to be expected.

Next morning we blancoed and polished our equipment and boots, shouldered our arms and marched sweatily through the brown August grass to Tidworth station where we intruded the smell of Brasso, boot-polish, straw, sweat and oily rifles into what was manifestly an ex-LSWR compartment though by that time marked 'Southern Railway'. There was a long wait at Ludgershall station while the hot sun glared in through the window before we chuffed off behind an ex-LSWR Jumbo to Waterloo.

There was also a 'holiday camp' organised by one of the masters on the Modern Side. It was non-military and those who attended it did so at his invitation. As I was not on the Modern Side and had never spoken to him before I was pleased, and rather flattered, when he stopped me one day in the playground and asked me if I'd like to attend it. The camp was near Harlow, in Essex (long before the New Town was thought up), by the side of the river Stort, and fishing was one of the attractions. I was delighted when I one day caught a trout with my homemade fishing rod. Bathing was another and we were encouraged to bathe naked, though the master himself didn't. One strict rule, however, was that we mustn't talk after Lights Out, and the master used to creep round outside the tents and listen through the brailing to make sure this rule was obeyed. At one point he told me I needed a bath, required me to parade at what purported to be the 'medical tent', undress and wash myself while he watched and asked questions. Although still fairly undeveloped I sensed that this interest in my cleanliness was merely ostensible. He made no passes at me but one night he overheard some – entirely innocent – talking in our tent and the next day Gibson and I were required to go with him to a hidden corner of a neighbouring field where our punishment was carried out: three swipes of the cane. As we were wearing only light summer shorts it hurt like hell and I could tell that it was out of all proportion to the crime. He was doing it for his own pleasure, not out of any sense of justice.

He was sailing very close to the wind. I never heard from any of the fellows that they'd been 'approached', nor was there, to my knowledge, any scandal but the possibility of it seemed to lie ahead. A lot could in any case go on without anyone breathing a word about it, usually to avoid embarrassment. I said nothing to my parents and the same no doubt went for the other boys. A year or two later one of Chilton's morning announcements was that he'd died, very young – and officially much lamented – though I privately felt it to be poetic justice.

I now find myself wondering whether in fact he committed suicide. In these more sophisticated days boys, parents, and fellow-masters would all regard a master who held such a camp with a certain suspicion but I think it very likely that Chilton, in particular, was something of an innocent in such matters. Words like 'homosexual', 'sadist', 'masochist' etc. mostly came in with Freud and Havelock Ellis in the twentieth century, well after Chilton's time at the university, and until there was a word for it, the phenomenon it represented remained largely unrecognised. Even now, however, I disapprove. Sadism does in fact strike me as something of a perversion but, be that as it may, all sexual activity requires mutual understanding and consent; it should not be obtained on false pretences, especially from the young.

In the summer of 1927, along with about a hundred others – several thousand over the whole kingdom – I had to sit for the Schools Certificate, with my fingers crossed, perhaps, but less tensely than might have been expected; certainly less tensely than Papa's. As we had to wait some weeks to know the result let me likewise keep the reader waiting and talk about an event which was much nearer the forefront of my mind: a visit to 'the Continent'.

Broader Horizons

Trips to the Continent are now so commonplace that one is surprised to recall how exceptional they were sixty years ago, except for a few, and it was not so much a matter of money as of habit. 'Holidays', at all events for middle-class families with children, meant 'the seaside' and they were often very conservative about it; 'We always go to Frinton/Swanage/ Cornwall, etc'. As for the workers, if they could afford a holiday it would be Brighton, Southend-on-Sea, Blackpool, and the like, and London ones often went hop-picking in Kent. Switzerland was in few people's thoughts. As for Spain, it was a country of exceptional foreignness which hardly anyone visited. One could certainly go to Thomas Cook's and get them to organize a tour but package tourism had scarcely been invented and the average Briton tended to regard even France with some suspicion; there was the language difficulty for a start, and French drinking water was not to be trusted.

It was entirely typical of Papa that he was not so conservative. At the age of eighteen he'd made a trip to see the Paris Exhibition of 1889 and had been among the first to ascend the Eiffel Tower. Again in 1901 he'd gone on a cycling tour of Holland, Westphalia and Belgium with his brother John. They'd needed no passports, he told us, nor any foreign exchange; they simply took a few gold sovereigns and pedalled off. It was at the time of the Boer War and for him a memorable incident had been that children in Brussels shouted '*A bas les anglais!*' at them. It will have enhanced his political awareness and I fancy that a later holiday, in St Valery-en-Caux, when Pen was two and I unborn, was influenced by the fact of the *Entente Cordiale*. It was therefore not surprising that when he saw the announcement of what was in effect a package tour arranged by the 'Free Church Touring Guild' he jumped at the chance, and again Politics will have influenced his choice. Geneva, the head office of the League of Nations, was much in the news, and in 1927 Monsieur Briand and Herr Stresemann were having talks which seemed to augur a great improvement in Franco-German relations. Such a holiday would be appropriate to the Better World which it was still hoped would be built on the ruins of the 1914–18 disaster.

He will, however, have had other considerations in mind, one no doubt being that since he'd been paying for a decade to have me taught French, he might see a return on his money by getting me to use it. He'd always regretted his own inability to speak any foreign language. Another probably was that, since we now had wealthy neighbours, we might as well 'keep up with the Rowsells' by appearing to have an expensive holiday though in fact it was less expensive than Scotland would have been. The Pound Sterling was a strong currency, far stronger than the French Franc. Swiss Francs were eighteen to the Pound. Switzerland in any case had a good image for being predominantly a Protestant country and I don't doubt that he will have felt it an advantage to have Free Church, hence like-minded, people as fellow-tourists though the fact that they were English-speakers will also have been in his mind.

My own feelings of anticipation were somewhat overshadowed by having to sit for the Schools Certificate (though I don't recall burning much midnight oil for it) but I nevertheless felt a tremor of excitment when our passports arrived, one of them taking official cognisance of me with a very bad photograph, and I noted that Sir Austen Chamberlain requested and required in the name of His Majesty all those whom it might concern to allow me to pass freely without let or hindrance and afford me every assistance and protection of which I might stand in need. Apart from that, indeed rather enhanced by that, I had chiefly in mind the railway aspect of the journey. It would be a new experience to take that non-stop Boat Train from Victoria to Newhaven, to say nothing of embarking on a boat, crossing the Channel and discovering that unknown quantity: French Railways.

Excitement comes of its own accord when, on a hot July morning, in the company of hundreds of others, one reaches the station, finds the right platform and gets into the waiting train, and mine continued as our Boat Train slipped through familiar Croydon and Purley and then, with sudden unfamiliarity, skirted Coulsdon North and entered the tunnel just beyond it, formerly seen only from Coulsdon South, on through the cutting and the other Merstham tunnel – unfamiliar views of familiar places – finally emerging at Earlswood. After that it was all unfamiliar but in the blazing July sunshine it continued exciting; the smell of oil on salt water; the smell of cooking in the boat; the smooth blue-green sea; coming alongside in Dieppe; going through a very perfunctory Customs and finally being let loose on the platform among several waiting trains.

After that it wasn't so much excitement as acute interest. Everything was so fascinatingly different. You couldn't see into the compartments properly because the platform was only about six inches high! And the only way into the carriage was by a door at the end with some very steep steps to be climbed. Moreover the French still had three classes and when I saw the bare wood of the 3rd class I felt relieved that our package entitled us to 2nd. Once we'd finally clambered in and settled down we found ourselves alongside a street of shops and some little boys came and tried to cadge cigarettes. 'Street urchins', it seemed, but I was struck by the beautiful way they pronounced the word '*cigarette*'; their speech seemed strangely at odds with their appearance and behaviour; no London street urchin would use such pure vowels. I then became conscious of a smell which I later identifed as Gauloise cigarettes (even now the smell of 'France'). I was in 'a foreign country'! If I'd had any cigarettes I'd certainly have given them some but at a very youthful sixteen (alas for lost innocence!) I hadn't yet become a smoker.

Thereafter impressions piled in unceasingly: the rich Normandy countryside with short-horned brindled cattle chewing the cud between the trees of orchards; Rouen, where Joan of Arc had been burned alive; going to the *toilette* at the end of the carriage and discovering that French urine apparently smelt stronger than English; the enormous size of our locomotive, with its pipes and snifting valves, when seen from ground level at St Lazare station; the incessant noisy honking of the traffic in the streets of Paris; having an evening meal at a table on the pavement outside a restaurant!, with much uncertainty about what the menu really meant and a consequent not-very-nice piece of red beef; the Gare de Lyon with trains announcing the most incredible destinations – Rome, Naples, Vienna, Budapest, Constantinople – and a hubbub of excited foreigners chattering on all sides in various languages; stopping in the middle of a very hot night at a place called Laroche-Mignonne where we had a change of engines and Father and I managed to get a bottle of fizzy *limonade* to slake our raging thirsts, then tearing off into the night again – French trains seemed to go at incredible speed! – and waking the next morning at a place called Vallorbe where there was a long wait and another perfunctory Customs check; emerging at Lausanne station where we sat at a table on the platfrom! and ate delicious rolls and cherry jam and coffee; getting into another train for Martigny in the Rhone valley; changing there and climbing into a mountain train which would take us up to a place called Orsières . . . there was no end to these delights and discoveries though the most rapturous was reserved for the last lap to Orsières. The slow little mountain train – though not chugging; Swiss trains were all electric! – wended its way between bushes and flowers swarming with Marbled Whites, Swallow-tails, Jersey Tigers and other treasures which I knew only from my book and had never seen in England. 'Switzerland' seemed like the gateway to Paradise.

Our final destination was Champex and, once installed at the Hotel du Glacier, it was the human fauna which caught my attention; not only Swiss but Dutch, Belgian, even German! – and here I discovered a pocket of the past which had remained undisturbed. Despite my approval of the League of Nations and the efforts of Messrs Briand and Stresemann, in an unexamined piece of double-think Germans had somehow remained, if not 'wicked' at least somewhat dubious people, to be treated with caution; it had never penetrated my consciousness that they were flesh-and-blood human beings like ourselves. The discovery meant a conscious putting away of childish things and there was more to come.

The English people in our package were certainly 'like-minded', i.e. very like the people at church, and in any case a good deal older than I, hence boring, and although I fell in with their activities – climbing up to the Glacier d'Orny and spending a night in the *cabane* there, etc. – I instinctively looked about for someone more contemporary to talk to and, if possible, to try out my schoolboy French. I shortly became aware of a youth who might have satisfied these requirements except that he seemed a bit beyond my reach; not only very good-looking but dazzling for other reasons. On the tennis court opposite the hotel he played tennis with his brothers and although clearly the youngest he outshone them, returning services and exchanging net volleys with a speed which seemed to me miraculous. I knew I couldn't take him on at tennis, even if I'd brought my racket, which I hadn't. Nevertheless I was reluctant to abandon the possibility of knowing him and looked around for some other means of engineering it. At mealtimes he sat with his family and I noticed that his mother in particular had the same rather *distingué* appearance but his older sister, though she had the same family likeness, was a great deal more approachable; she chatted pleasantly to all comers and I looked out for opportunites of getting into conversation with her.

One possibility was music. The hotel guests used to assemble in the *salon* of an evening and, as in England, people 'brought their music' if they had any to bring. (Such was our pre-TV innocence!). One evening this family offered as their contribution Bach's '*Mon coeur croyant*' which Mother sometimes sang to the words 'My heart ever faithful' and I could see from their copy that the German was '*Mein glaübiges Herze*' though their version of it was an arrangement for two violins, played by my tennis-player and one of his brothers, with their sister – I'd discovered her name was Alice – at the piano. As one of the lady guests wanted an accompanist I volunteered to play for her, hoping that this might lead to an exchange of compliments, even – who knows? – to playing piano duets with Alice, but in this I was disappointed.

I therefore fell back on butterflies. I'd lost no opportunity of adding to my collection during hot afternoons in the valley below and the fact became known in the hotel; one lady declared an interest in seeing my collection. Catching sight of her in conversation with Alice one evening I seized my chance so that Alice could admire them as well. She exclaimed, *'Ah, que c'est joli!'* in typically enraptured tones. (It occurred to no one, in those days, to criticize their capture on the grounds of Conservation.) From that moment I was 'in'. Alice chatted freely about her young brother, Eric; I learnt that he'd just missed becoming Junior Champion of French Switzerland and that he had two passions: *'Lire, et jouer au tennis.'* After that it was a short step to talking with their father, *un professeur*, who spoke French so distinctly and unhurriedly that I could understand every word. This was good for morale. Most people, when I addressed them in French, replied at a speed which disconcerted me. It was not only the speed; Eric's eldest brother turned out to be a naturalised Briton and his English wife, who was also of the party, spoke French at high speed but with such an English accent that I had no difficulty in following her though I suspected she did it on purpose, not wanting to be thought anything but English. This struck me as extraordinary. I should have been delighted to be mistaken for a native and lost no opportunity of improving my accent as a convincing camouflage. Casting off an English one was also putting away childish things.

The first time I talked to Eric, therefore, we discussed 'literature' but my knowledge of French literature, apart from reading Victor Hugo in translation, was confined to what we'd studied at school – Merimée, Alphonse Daudet, Montesquieu – and he spoke little English so we didn't get very far. I did however learn that his mother was German, the daughter of a Lutheran parson, and was deeply impressed by the knowledge. Germans were not only human beings; some of them were serious Christians! I was even pleased that he was a Protestant, not because I took religion so seriously but because it seemed to make him easier to know than if he'd been a Catholic. At the end of the holiday we exchanged addresses and promised to write to one another; a normal end to a holiday but for me a serious promise. I had in fact fallen in love and was more or less aware of it, having previously fallen for the leader of the gymn team at school, an undeclared affection which would have embarrassed its object had he been aware of it but nevertheless a large step towards putting away childish things. (Eric in fact became my greatest friend and his death in 1982 was another thing which prompted these recollections.)

Remembering the tremendous impact made on me by 'Europe' on that first visit in 1927 I feel astonished when the contemporary young can take their holidays there and come back unimpressed – except by the cheapness of the wine or some such detail – and with their horizons quite unbroadened, and the same happens in reverse. The sight of parties of French and Italian young, recently, visiting this country for the first time, suggested part of the answer: they come in gangs and they go about in gangs. Well, I went with a gang, admittedly much more middle-aged than I so that I felt estranged from them with their 'trendy' urge towards 'Community Singing' (in English, of course) or Folk Dancing, most of which rather embarrassed me. It wasn't difficult to dissociate myself from such a scene but it was a warning against Package Tourism; if you want to get the best of of new circumstances you should know what you're after and pursue it single-mindedly. That the Free Church Tourists occupied their time by assembling in their private *salon* in a separate chalet, and singing 'The Road to the Isles' or dancing 'Sellenger's Round' or 'Rufty-Tufty' suggested that travel, far from broadening their minds, had made them feel more insular and inclined to feel that British is Best, and any foreigners who heard or saw them will have been conscious of their insularity. It did less than nothing to improve international relations and in fact contributed to my estrangement from church. Nice people, no doubt, but I reckoned I could do better than that. I'd been introduced to the ways of the Continent and realised that in future I'd be able to get around it on my own. I did in fact accompany my parents on another package to the Italian Lakes a year or two later but that was the end of package tourism for me, and even at Champex I often got away on my own to catch butterflies around Orsieres.

Those exquisitely-coloured, velvety fantasies seemed proof of the existence of God, 'divine creation'. Even if one could accept that they'd evolved for some utilitarian purpose – as their undersides evidently had, for camouflage – nevertheless what inventiveness! Flight, too, was another godlike capacity, applying also to birds who in addition had the capacity to utter sounds. Part of the magic of butterflies, however, was their inscrutable silence; they appeared out of nowhere, like visions, and then, when the sun went in, disappeared into nowhere again, and Switzerland, with its diversity of climates, could boast varieties unknown in Britain. The setting in which they did so was another experience; above me was Mont Catogne, steeper than any mountain I'd ever seen before, and under the bright blue sky beyond it lay 'Italy'. I was conscious that Life lay ahead and it seemed an inviting prospect.

What felt like the apotheosis of these romantic sentiments came one hot afternoon when, feeling very thirsty, I went into the sole, rather modest, cafe-bar which Orsières provided and in my best French accent asked for '*Du vin, s'il vous plait*'. The girl, no doubt spotted an innocent abroad but nevertheless asked politely '*Un demi-litre?*' thereby reminding me that I'd no idea how much half-a-litre amounted to. I said '*Oui*, in a tone of voice which tried to suggest that this was just about the modest quantity I wanted. She served it in a carafe, a local dry white wine, no doubt from the Rhone valley, just down the line. Never having drunk wine before I also had no idea what effect nearly a pint of the stuff would have on me but after a few mouthfuls euphoria set in. I was the only client in the place. Orsières was a rustic hamlet consisting of a few chalets and farm buildings surrounded by heaps of cow-dung, and its cafe-bar can seldom have been crowded but, no doubt for this reason, the girl was pleased to talk and asked me about my butterflies. I was delighted to tell her and to answer other questions about myself which followed and, thanks to the wine, felt I was becoming positively fluent. I had more difficulty understanding what she said than in formulating my own sentences. I heard a word which I visualised as *'cellement'* and tried to think what it meant until it suddenly dawned on me that she'd said *'seulement'* but all this was the stuff of learning. In the euphoric haze which shortly descended on me I had a sudden moment of truth: Good heavens! I'm in Switzerland and I'm sitting drinking wine and talking French to a native! and felt proud of myself.

Thanks, perhaps, to my concentration while drinking, that pint of wine didn't lay me out though as a raw beginner it might well have done. When I finally got out into the hot August sunshine I realised that I was a bit drunk but felt proud of myself for that too. The way up to Champex was a very steep and sweaty climb but at least it had the effect of sobering me down and once back in the Hotel du Glacier I was quite myself again, indeed rather more than my previous self. I felt I'd made great strides towards growing up but said nothing to my parents. That too was part of growing up.

Yet another was ballroom dancing. Twice a week a dance-band visited the hotel and I had the novel experience of inviting charming girls to take the floor with me. I'd had a few lessons at home but this was the first time I'd put them to the test, meanwhile trying to make conversation in French though the nationality of the girls varied. One evening two American girls turned up and I had a lesson in *savoir faire*; I asked one of them to dance and, when she declined, asked her friend, whereupon it was explained ot me that this was impolite. 'We don't do that back home', she said. There, if a girl declined, the man had to accept the fact and sit the dance out; he mustn't move on to the next girl as much as to say 'You'll do'. I was unable to tell her whether the same applied in England as I simply didn't know. According to Mama you couldn't ask a girl to dance unless you'd been introduced to her in which case you bowed and said 'May I have the pleasure?' but this evidently didn't apply in Switzerland. There you could ask any girl you liked to dance, saying simply *'Voulez-vous danser?'* and it was bad form for her to refuse.

Nearly all the tunes were American, and top of the pops in Champex that year was 'YOU . . . stole my heart away' (still eminently retrievable). If I heard it again now, especially played by saxophone, piano, double bass and clumping drums, it would bring the Hotel du Glacier with its creaking pine-boards, in 1927, vividly alive again. I find another tune being unearthed alongside it: *'Wenn die weisse Flieder · wieder blüht'*. Does it belong there? . . . or to Stuttgart in 1929? Secreted in the same pocket of memory is 'Ramona', plonked out on a barrel-organ in Bloomsbury, and that, I know belongs to 1928 and is associated with 'Eric' and a pre-Hitler Europe now unbelievably remote.

I returned to England with my head full of 'Europe' and of my beautiful, French-speaking, half-German friend, and with Father pleased that the holiday had turned out a success. He'd certainly seen his expenditure on French rewarded; when we had a meal in Paris on the way home I was required to deal with the waiter and felt even more grown-up. Back at school I became one of Tootsies' best pupils, and pleased Oakley, the form-master of the Sixth, by my even more enthusiastic support for the League of Nations Union. I don't recall pleasing Ellingham by anything in particular, except that the results of the School Certificate showed that I'd passed with credits in French, English and Maths. No doubt he felt that I should have got credits in Latin and Greek – as no doubt I should – but at least I could now move up to the Sixth Form, enter the school by the august front entrance on the Victoria Embankment, be one of those who ranged themselves in an arc behind Chilton at prayers and generally give myself the airs of a young man, 'daily further from the east'.

The light of common day, however, lay ahead and Father was a good deal more exercised about it than I was. 'The university' was considered but depended on my getting a scholarship. I sat for one but didn't get it and don't recall that this was much of a surprise to anyone. Father may even have been a little relieved as it would only have produced £50 a year though he'd certainly have stretched himself if I'd shown any sign of an academic bent or evinced a strong desire for a particular career. As I did neither he decided to do what he'd probably always hoped for and got me into insurance where he had plenty of good contacts. In the City, however, the Schools Certificate had far less prestige than the London Matriculation, though there was little to choose between them. If I'd got five credits in the former it would have given me exemption from the latter. As I'd only got three, nothing would do but I must sit for 'Matric' in the following January.

Daily Further from the East

The next two terms were a kind of interim between boyhood and manhood. At school the freedom of the Sixth allowed time for private study of the set books for the Matric with Oakley as my 'tutor'. Oakley was the nicest man alive and the very antithesis of a man like Gardener; one of the few, in fact, who'd absorbed the lessons of 'the war' and felt some effort should be made to try to turn the world into a better place, but also a serious and thoughtful scholar who gave me an insight into what a university might be like. He expected one to be a knowledgeable and reflective student who would 'read' on his own account, out of interest, rather than a pupil who merely did what he was told, though he gave valuable advice on what to read – and being in the Sixth gave one the privilege of using the school library.

My studies continued through the Christmas vacation. Father found me a crammer, a master at Reigate Grammar School, to whose house I repaired two or three times a week; and an abiding memory of that blessed interim is getting there. This was the winter of 1927/8 when on Boxing Day a tremendous snowstorm disrupted communications throughout the kingdom, so I put on knee-breeches and trudged the four miles of stockbroker belt through snow that had drifted in places to two or three feet deep. A snowy landscape was also a little 'out of this world'.

Even sitting for the exam had a certain enchantment. It was held at the Imperial Institute in South Kensington and was spread over several days so that, for the first time in my life, I spent nights in London. Pen, by now married, lived in a 'flat' – another new experience – at the corner of Beaufort Street,

Chelsea, and I daily walked to the Institute and back. I enjoyed the novel experience and was a little surprised at my own unworriedness. The possibility of failing barely seemed to enter my head, and back at the flat I enjoyed the equally novel sensation of looking out of an upstairs drawing-room window and seeing the street below and the back gardens of the houses on the other side of Kings Road. One evening, when the exam was over, my brother-in-law had a few friends in, thrust a glass of Tollemache into my hand and told me to drink it. It was the first time I'd ever tasted beer but although I felt grown-up for drinking it I didn't really like it. It seemed to me horribly bitter.

Much more to my liking was a gramophone record he had of a Beethoven string quartet (Theme & Variations from Op. 18, No. 5) played by the Catterall String Quartet. The gramophone was becoming increasingly respectable and I found I could fall for a piece of music as one falls in love. I went crazy about these variations and once put the record on six times in succession, loving it more each time, unworried by the fact that the machine had to be wound up by hand and the needle changed at the end of each side (and one side of a – very heavy and fragile – bakelite record only lasted four minutes). What was recorded was much governed by its length, or its divisibility, and pieces were sometimes treated with a Procrustean high-handedness. Uncle John had a record of Cortot playing Chopin's Ballade in G minor, which had also been a source of rapture, but when I bought the book of Ballades in order to try and play it myself I discovered that roughly the first third of it had been *cut* so that the dazzling remainder could be squeezed into two sides of one record!

The Beethoven Variations could be divided fairly neatly into two so that the enforced interval while one turned the record over, changed the needle, and wound up the machine was hardly noticed. ('Electrical recording' was just coming in but it seems almost incredible, at this distance, to recall that 'long play' records, at 33 rpm, didn't come in until about 1950.) A woman in the flat above frequently broadened my horizons with a fascinatingly different piece of music for piano which I later discovered to be the Passepied from Debussy's Suite Bergamasque. (To hear that now would bring Chelsea, 1928, back alive and at the age of seventeen one's horizons are wonderfully broadenable. Late in life one chiefly deepens appreciation of the already known.)

Back at school I ticked over, pending the results of the Matric, and extended my range by studying Spanish with a fellow named Benzies. We had no instruction; we simply got it out of a Spanish grammar and took it in turns to hear each other, finding most of it fairly easy thanks to its similarity to Latin and French. Then the Matric results appeared. Father came home from the office one evening with a copy of the Times under his arm and from the good-humoured look on his face I felt sure I must have passed. He didn't deny it, allowed me to look for myself and there, for the first time in my life, was my name in the papers. That settled it; I was due for the City and before long went for an interview at an Insurance Office and was accepted – at an initial salary of £70 a year. I docilely accepted all this. I'd nothing better to suggest and the prospect of earning money, even so small an amount of it, had its attractions, as did the prospect of shedding the school cap and wearing a bowler or, in summer, a straw boater.

I finally left school at short notice, thereby letting down a theatrical producer (was his name Lloyd James?) who'd cast me as Viola in a performance of *Twelfth Night* due to take place in the Great Hall. With my new preoccupations I hardly gave this a thought at the time but gave it several thereafter. If it had been a great success it might have made clearer what I was good at, though I was slow to read the signs, being inclined to underrate what came easily to me. I'd won prizes for speaking Shakespeare's lines and in previous years earned good notices for acting ability but it never occurred to me that I might have potential as an actor. If it had, my career might have been less of a problem, and if I'd sufficiently impressed Lloyd James, who was connected with the London theatre, I might have become a famous actor! It would certainly have been more in my line than insurance clerking but 'the Stage' was never so much as considered by anyone in my environment.

When I finally took my leave of the masters, Oakley in particular gave the impression that he felt it to be 'such a pity' that I was merely going to the City when I ought to have been headed for higher things, no doubt thinking of the university. As Father was the only one to have ideas on the subject it was natural that his prevailed. I could at least earn my living until I got ideas myself though it was a couple of years before any emerged. I'd taken up water-colours in my spare time (in an effort to impress Eric) and at an exhibition given by a society of local artists, not only won two prizes but was later amazed to learn that I'd sold two pictures, at two guineas a time, to a rich American who'd bought them off the wall without knowing anything else about me. After that I wanted to take up Art as a career but by that time we were in deep Depression; it was no moment to throw up a perfectly good, if boring, job and embark on the precarious career of 'artist' and Father naturally wouldn't hear of it.

So, the end of childhood and emergence into the light of common day. In my own thoughts and in my spare time I was conscious of travelling daily further from the east and became increasingly wrapped up in my own activities, giving my parents less and less of my confidence while continuing to have arguments with them over the meal table. Religion was sometimes a *casus belli* but almost any subject would serve to suggest to Father that he was old-fashioned and that a younger generation knew better. He may have wondered privately whether I was right but nevertheless defended himself vigorously. One day, however, in a less contentious atmosphere, I asked him why he continued to go to church every Sunday, even though he'd admitted freely to 'honest doubt'. He said he felt it to be a good habit to withdraw himself from worldly affairs once a week and lift his eyes unto the hills. It was a perfectly sound reason – always provided it achieved its object – but my own attendance at church services gave me no such sense of liberation or exaltation; I found them increasingly irksome. That hymn of Tennyson's contained the line 'And more of reverence in us dwell' and it was that very 'reverence', especially as displayed by Mama – to the tune by John Bacchus

Dykes – which brought out the rebel in me. I was further repelled by a letter I received about that time from the minister of the church which seemed to embody what I felt I was up against:

> 'Just a line to give you our hearty greeting on the commencement of another chapter in your life.
>
> As a young warrior, his face toward the glamoured future steps forth gallantly and with superb confidence to the great adventure, it is perhaps a minor significance to him that loving eyes are watching, and lips moving in prayer for him, but someday he will recall the fact, and then perchance it will be a source of comfort to him, and maybe an inspiration stirring him to finer effort that the faith and hope of those old friends shall be justified.
>
> Anyhow we want you to know our good wishes go with you as you sail out of School Bay and make for the Open Sea. We are confident you will succeed, and equally confident that you will worthily uphold the fine traditions associated with the terms 'Christian' and 'Gentleman'.
>
> I fear the younger generation is beginning to regard me as a "Back Number" but if ever there should be an occasion on which you think I could perhaps render you some service, I hope you will do me the honour of giving me your confidence and allowing me to try and help.
>
> Meanwhile hearty congratulations, and best wishes from
>
> Your ever sincere friend ...

It was what I felt to be the 'Victorianness' of this letter which repelled me, and in the 1920s the Victorians were coming under heavy fire. Lytton Strachey had discharged one of the earliest salvos in 1918 with his 'Eminent Victorians' and followed it up with 'Queen Victoria' in 1921. Debunking them became fashionable and a good deal of bunk was still in circulation. There was also the negative bunk – in uncirculation – of 'not thinking certain thoughts'. In tune with my time I was beginning to lap up three very different authors who were essential reading for my generation: Aldous Huxley, D.H.

Lawrence, and Ernest Hemmingway, all of them – seen in the context of what had gone before which is the only way new authors can be seen – writing more frankly about sex than any novelists had had the courage to do for more than a century, but all of them greeted with feelings of outrage by my parents' generation, though the likelihood was that they'd no more than dip into them, whilst feeling virtuous for not contaminating themselves further. These authors had not only defied the convention of not thinking certain thoughts; they'd dared to publish those thoughts, thereby endangering the morals of the young. D.H. Lawrence was a particular object of their obloquy.

My office had an arrangement with Mudies Library whereby one of the Messengers went every morning to the library in Old Broad Street with our late borrowings and returned there in the afternoon to collect new ones selected by the library staff from our request lists. Thanks to this I read all of Lawrence's available books, and thanks to a fellow at the office who'd smuggled in an unexpurgated copy of *Lady Chatterly's Lover* from Paris, I read that too. When I got home I normally left my current reading matter on the hall table and Father would often take a look at it to see what I was filling my head with. I think some of them impressed him but others – in one case some of Ezra Pound's 'Cantos' – scandalised him and if it hadn't been a library book he'd probably have thrown it in the fire. I therefore soon learnt to keep any dubious books out of sight but even *Sons and Lovers* earned his disapproval, though for a different reason: Lawrence had exposed his own father's weaknesses to the public gaze. I expressed surprise, seeing that it was no more than the truth, but he reckoned that any decent son would keep quiet about such things. His own father, having died when he was ten years old, would have been beyond criticism and permanently prevented Father from seeing him as a human being, let alone talking to him as such.

One day in a bookshop in Old Broad Street I saw Lawrence's paper-backed essay *Pornography and Obscenity* and promptly bought a copy but hid it at the bottom of a drawer where my parents were unlikely to find it. In fact it was a fairly rational discussion of the subject which could have been discussed over the meal-table if such things hadn't been 'unmentionable'. (It is now a Collector's Piece but alas I no longer possess it; when I was away at the war, some years later, Mother had a spring cleaning, discovered it at the bottom of my drawer, and promptly burnt it – natually without reading it.)

Mother, or her presence, was part of the difficulty. Such things couldn't be discussed in the presence of women. Father on his own, in a man-to-man mood, could be rather more realistic though even then he was worried about the effect on me. He, too preferred on the whole to put such things out of his mind. He once admitted to having seen some pornographic postcards at the office and wished he'd never done so. He'd even, I discovered, once read some Havelock Ellis but said that after a bit you felt you'd been 'wallowing in filth'. He'd inherited a tradition of Progress and 'making the world a better place to live in'. The message of Shaw's Life Force in *Back to Methusaleh*: 'a power that seeks to raise mankind, with their cooperation, to a higher and better existence' was potent with him but this lifting of one's eyes unto the hills – especially with less intelligent men than he – could all-too-readily be the obverse of sweeping anything unpleasant under the carpet. It could also lead to dressing up things pleasant as more beautiful/noble/sacred than they really were. The letter from the minister, with its talk of 'the young warrior' and 'the glamoured future' when the occasion was a mere hum-drum leaving school and getting a job as an insurance clerk, was quite a good example.

As for the presence of women, he'd though about this too and was sympathetic towards the Feminist movement but he took it for granted that women must remain 'pure'; equality of the sexes could not possibly mean that women might be 'immoral' in the way that men had been allowed to get away with it in the past, and it therefore followed that men must remain pure too. Needless to say Mother and her sisters strongly endorsed this view. Tennyson's 'Sir Galahad' had already been promoted into a hero figure, and G.F. Watts, that melodramtic painter so much in vogue in their youth, had painted a picture of him fighting the dragon of impurity – 'My strength is as the strength of ten Because my heart is pure'. As the first male born into that oppressively female family since their little brother John in the 1890s – himself pretty unique in being the solitary male after eight sisters – I was material for their development. They'd already had some success in making me a pianist, and later a tenor. To make me also a true Sir Galahad would be their crowing achievement, a kind of fin-de-siecle artefact.

It was chiefly the influence of this monstrous regiment of women that I was rebelling against and I fought back on all fronts, determined to be myself and not what they wanted to make me. Though inevitably young and ignorant – and half-aware of it – I was nevertheless quick to pounce on ignorance in others. Thanks to my long daily train journies – and to Mudies' Library – I was making up for the lack of university education by doing a great deal of reading, and the erudition of such writers as Aldous Huxley provided me with numerous moments when I could show myself 'one up', especially as my parents didn't do a great deal of reading themselves. Huxley, who held a high place in my pantheon – and of many others besides – had a way of referring casually to authors, artists, poets, as if you knew all about their work; every educated person did. I didn't but I wasted no time in finding out, adding their names to my library list and generally repairing the lacunae. Knowledge was an appetite that grew with what it fed on but the effortless display of it in Huxley was an early aperitif.

I gave little thought to what a bumptious young puppy I must sometimes appear but all the time I was in fact slowly learning from both my parents whose example, as well as their words, brought me up inter alia to think well of other people. This admittedly had a negative counterpart of assuming that others would be well-disposed towards me and the discovery, the hard way, that both these assumptions could be mistaken caused me a good deal of pain and grief in later life but I now feel that to think well of other people is the right approach. One learns to be alert to the possibility of their proving guilty, but to behave as if assuming their innocence, while keeping a sharp eye open, usually gets better results.

As for the influence of religion, my mistaken assumptions were probably further compounded by ancestral voices murmuring 'God is Good'. It was a piece of received Truth, seemingly the message of the Universe, and since for much of my early life 'God' was identified with 'Father', and Father was unquestionably a good man, I unconsciously believed in human goodness to a far greater extent than the evidence warranted. To some extent this was a Victorian legacy and fairly widely shared; I fancy Neville Chamberlain was duped by Hitler partly because his upbringing and experience had disinclined him to believe that such evil men as Hitler could exist, at all events in high places and, *mutatis mutandis,* much the same could be said about Lenin, Stalin, and a multitude of other devils that the twentieth century has produced in such large numbers. One is tempted to think that this apparent surge of devilry stems from the cessation of a belief in God but the historical evidence doesn't seem to point that way. Western Civilisation became immensely more civilised when uncertainty and agnosticism made it tolerant. The devils were nearly always those who were quite sure that they *knew,* that they were *right,* and so tolerated no other ideas than their own. The Inquisition could be just as devilish on God's behalf as those like Lenin, who were cocksure that God did not exist, and therefore that the end justified the means, however immoral.

One may well doubt, however, whether Hitler, Lenin, *et al* were brought up to the tune of 'Surely goodness and mercy shall follow me all the days of my life', or to consider that the very hairs of their heads might be all numbered, and belief in Something usually tends to make people more moral provided that Something is not too explicitly expressed. It was in fact thanks to Aldous Huxley that I first saw 'religion' from quite a different viewpoint. He published a book called *Texts and Pretexts,* an anthology of poems with his own perceptive comments added. Most of them were new to me and one poet in particular, Walt Whitman, adumbrated a conception that Something which chiefly consisted in saying what it is not:

> The sun and stars that float in the open air,
> The apple-shaped earth and we upon it – surely the drift of them is something grand!
> I do not know what it is except that it is grand and it is happiness,
> And that the enclosing purpose of us here is not a speculation, or bon mot, or reconnaissance,
> And that it is not something which by luck may turn out well for us and without luck must be a failure for us,
> And not something which may yet be retracted in a certain contingency

One might extend Voltaire's apothegm and assert that if God were not Good it would nevertheless be necessary to regard Him so. To believe Him to be malign would make nonsense of creation, despite its disturbing redness in tooth and claw. That the hairs of our heads should be all numbered sounds like an arresting metaphor, not intended to be taken too literally, yet the researches of recent decades with electron microscopes and radar-telescopes in micro- and macro-cosmic fields of physics and biology make it seem very much less far-fetched. It seems clear that we, and the planet we live on, form part and parcel of a mutli-dimensional Whole so very much greater as to be impossible for us to conceive – fully to imagine a 'light year' is difficult enough – yet we can feel sure that we belong to it and, in that sense, matter. The exact nature of our importance we neither know nor need to know. To be preoccupied with one's own personal survival – as Tolstoy was; a spoilt boy whose upbringing made him full of his own importance – is to be importunate, to want to be noticed, in the way I tried with Ellingham.

At the age of seventeen, however, one is seldom much worried by thoughts of personal survival; Death is too far off to enter into one's calculations. Much more preoccupying, when one happens across it, is Love, a Fire from Heaven which while it lasts transforms one's existence and, even if it burns itself out, leaves one a different person.